D1116107

THE EMERGENCE OF IMPERIAL JAPAN

Self-Defense or Calculated Aggression?

DS
881.9
,M33
c.2

952.03
M41e
C.2

PROBLEMS IN ASIAN CIVILIZATIONS

THE EMERGENCE OF IMPERIAL JAPAN

Self-Defense or Calculated Aggression?

EDITED WITH AN INTRODUCTION BY

Marlene J. Mayo

UNIVERSITY OF MARYLAND

D. C. HEATH AND COMPANY

Lexington, Massachusetts

Copyright © 1970 by D. C. Heath and Company

All rights reserved. No part of this publication may be reproduced or transmitted in any form or by any means, electronic or mechanical, including photocopy, recording, or any information storage or retrieval system, without permission in writing from the publisher.

Printed in the United States of America

Library of Congress Number: 79–108789

CONTENTS

Introduction   vii

Conflict òf Opinion   xv

PROLOGUE   i
Oka Yoshitake

I.   ANCIENT DREAMS AND PRESENT FEARS

Robert T. Pollard
Traditional Expansionism   13

Hyman Kublin
Response to Western Aggression   19

W. G. Beasley
A Question of Timing and Not of Goals   25

II.   EXPANSION BY FORCE AND DIPLOMACY

John M. Maki
Lingering Militarism   31

M. Frederick Nelson
The Confucian World Order   35

James Crowley
Requirements of National Security   39

III.   NATIONALISM AND EXPANSIONISM

E. Herbert Norman
Ultranationalist Societies   47

Marius Jansen
Pan-Asianism   55

Matsumoto Sannosuke
National Mission   59

IV.   THE ECONOMIC ARGUMENT

O. Tanin and E. Yohan
Capitalism and Imperialism   69

Fujii Shōichi
*Capitalism, International Politics, and
the Emperor System*   75

HILARY CONROY
A Rebuttal to Economic Determinism   83

V.   PREMEDITATED MURDER OR ACCIDENTAL DEATH

GEORGE KERR
Blueprint for Conquest   89

HILARY CONROY
Unexpected Happenings   95

SUGGESTIONS FOR ADDITIONAL READING   101

INTRODUCTION

IN the long reign of the Meiji Emperor, 1868–1912, Japan became a modern state, an empire, and a world power. In succession, Japan settled Hokkaido, incorporated the Ryukyu Islands and the Bonins, extended its jurisdiction over the Kuriles, set up a colonial administration in Formosa, acquired a leasehold and economic concessions in southern Manchuria, took over the southern part of Sakhalin, and annexed Korea. By 1910 these amazing advances had provoked a few cries of alarm in Europe and America, but they were muffled by the general chorus of praise for Japan's civilizing influence in East Asia. Then Japan seemed to cross the vague boundary between benevolent and correct expansionism on one side and malevolent and irrational imperialism on the other. International approval turned into condemnation as Japan continued to enlarge its empire, only to lose it all in the disaster of 1945.

Most accounts of this spectacular tale tend to gloss over the early stages of Japan's expansion and place more emphasis on the origins of the Greater East Asia War and the attack on Pearl Harbor. There are books on Japan "before aggression" and "after imperialism," but no single comprehensive work on Japan's adoption of imperialism. This may reflect the widespread belief that the explanation in Japan's case is really very simple. In one view, for example, modern Japan was heir to a long tradition of militarism and expansionism and so found it easy to imitate the behavior of the threatening imperialist West at the turn of the century. Or, as economic determinists would say, empire was a logical result of Japan's capitalist industrialization. Both views, however, take for granted a great deal that is unknown or unproved about Japanese history and national character, and they help little in understanding Japan's motives. In the Meiji period, Japan somehow managed simultaneously to acquire an empire and undergo modernization while other Asian empires and peoples declined in a world collapsed under Western pressure. How this came about deserves study on its own terms. But it also deserves attention as a contribution to comparative history, for Japan's experience with imperialism is no less significant than that of European countries and the United States. Attention to Japan's case may help define better the relationship between capitalism and empire and the workings of international politics.

The selections in this volume have therefore been chosen to illustrate Meiji expansionism. What happened after the annexation of Korea in 1910 requires separate analysis, for World War I and the Chinese and Russian revolutions created new complications in Japan's foreign relations at a time when power was shifting to new groups. The questions here are not why the Twenty-One Demands in 1915, or Mukden in 1931, or Pearl Harbor in 1941. They are why the incorporation of the Ryukyu Islands back in 1872, the expedition to Taiwan in 1874, and the acquisition of Formosa in 1895. Although the literature dealing with Japan is thin by comparison with the many volumes on Western imperialism, enough of importance has now been said to outline the major problems, provoke argument, and encourage further research. The selections included here reflect a wide range of opinion and represent Japanese and Western scholarship before and after World War II.

To formulate the problem of Japan's modern empire in this volume as an either/or proposition of self-defense or systematic aggression may seem arbitrary. And merely to rephrase the alternative viewpoints—a response to Western aggression or a revival of traditional expansionism—does not eliminate grounds for such criticism. But in neither case are the propositions simply an artificial device to manufacture debate. Whether or not they are seen as equally false alternatives, they do represent the basic questions which the Japanese have asked of themselves and have been asked by their defenders and critics. Most of the authors of the selections included here accept one or the other contention even if preoccupied with a different theme. Either they emphasize the danger to Japan from the West and Japan's right, indeed duty, to defend itself, or they imply that Japanese imperialism was particularly ugly because it was calculating and bloodthirsty—just what one would expect of a basically military society. But precisely where in between these extremes does the truth lie?

An acceptable definition of imperialism is as much a problem when talking about Japan as about Britain or the United States. The word is employed for different purposes in propaganda, popular rhetoric, and scholarly treatises, and it is often used interchangeably with aggression and expansion. A few historians refuse to use the word at all, for it has become an automatic term of abuse, too closely bound up with communist criticism of capitalist societies or nationalist reaction to external influences. Most, however, do not regard the many connotations of imperialism as an invitation to abandon the term; rather they see them as a challenge for increased precision. As used here, imperialism is the extension of control over alien peoples and territories, whether by outright conquest or by economic and cultural penetration. It has existed in ancient and modern times, has been practiced in the eastern and western worlds, and is not unique to capitalist societies.

In general, historians of the far more carefully studied phenomenon of Western imperialism recognize a complicated interplay of causes and motives rather than accept a single cause as the sole explanation. Those who deal with Europe's age of discovery and early colonialism have drawn up a convenient catalogue of motives under the headings of god, gold, and glory. In discussions about the later imperialism of modern European states, during and after their transformation by the industrial revolution, these themes

have been recast as mission, profits, and power—or humanitarianism, capitalism, and nationalism. Without too much distortion, they can be transposed to the Japanese scene of the late nineteenth century as Pan-Asianism, capitalism, and Japanism. All of these are relevant, but scholars persist in trying to determine whether any of the interacting forces is dominant at a particular time or for all times, or in seeking still different explanations.

There is, to begin with, wide acceptance of a basically economic explanation: the need of capitalist industrial societies to find new markets, sources of raw materials, areas of investment, and outlets for surplus population. Arguments which do not reflect something of the Marxist-Leninist analysis of imperialism as the dying stage of capitalism would be regarded as naive, particularly by Japanese scholars. And at this late date in the twentieth century, to attribute imperialism in Japan or elsewhere to a collusion between business and military groups would be to say nothing novel either in the scholarship or folklore of imperialism. Few scholars, whether convinced Marxists or not, would deny the importance of economic causes, but not all would agree that they invariably outweigh other considerations or that capitalists as owners of the means of economic production automatically become makers of state policy. It is difficult to label Japan's first aggressive moves and wars as capitalistic when the dimensions of commerce and industry and the political influence of businessmen were inadequate to provide such motivation.

Recently, there has been a transfer of allegiance to another dominant theme which seems to offer a better key to understanding ancient and modern forms of imperialism: self-defense or national security. The security argument has been used, for example, to explain Han China's expansion into Central Asia in the second century B.C.—to discourage raids and invasions by nomadic tribes and not to engage in conquest for its own sake or promote commerce—and

Britain's growing involvement in Africa in the late nineteenth century—to defend the trade routes to India and not to exploit Africa. It has also been used to explain the American presence in Vietnam and the Russian interventions in Hungary and Czechoslovakia. The emphasis on security seems particularly pertinent to the case of Meiji Japan. Admittedly there was economic motivation, but above all there was anxiety about Japan's survival as an independent political and cultural entity as the West advanced further into Asia. Both the Meiji statesmen and their critics saw Japan existing precariously in a menacing, competitive world dominated by the power rivalries of aggressive Western peoples. Examination of the evidence may in fact show that Japan began to modernize just as there was a lull in the Western advance, that it was never in serious danger of a takeover, and that its statesmen on the whole were aware of this. Yet there was always the possibility of a renewed Western threat in more virulent form. Japan could not afford to be weak or unprepared. A modern military establishment and a solid industrial base were therefore necessary not to satisfy generals or to make profits but to give Japan the power to survive.

However, many Japanese believed that security also depended upon expansion and not merely a strong defense. In the last century of Tokugawa rule, when little was known of the outside world, critics of the government had demanded counter-aggression as a deterrent to Russian expansion. In the Meiji period, after knowledge of Asia and the West had considerably increased, there continued to be widespread acceptance of the axiom that the best defense is offense. Furthermore, some Japanese professed fear of living in an unstable area where the weakness of ones backward neighbors might tempt Western intervention. They expanded the right of self-defense to include the extension of control over surrounding areas and peoples. Japan, like the Western powers, must have an empire in order to protect itself and its interests. A classical expression of such

views was made in 1885 by Soejima Taneomi while rebuking a young patriot who thought Japan's chances of maintaining its independence could be improved by collaboration with an enlightened Korea. As foreign minister, 1871–73, Soejima had favored expeditions to Taiwan and Korea and had become a great favorite of critics of the government after resigning his post in 1873.

What kind of world do you think we live in? I call it a world where there is a struggle for power. Strong countries make it their business to conquer weak ones and constantly increase their territories. If life is a struggle, then our country must have adequate military strength to cope with this reality. Without military strength, we cannot survive. However civilized Korea becomes, do you think the great powers, who are as greedy as wild beasts, will decline to eat? On the contrary, the more civilized Korea becomes, the better feast it will make. . . . It is certain that the powers will choose a time that is best for them and annex Korea. Japan too faces the same danger. It is a country surrounded by the seas. In naval warfare, Japan is easy for the enemy to attack but hard for us to defend. Therefore, if we want to preserve Japan's independence permanently, we must possess territory on the continent. There are only two countries on the continent Japan can seize, China and Korea. Students with little experience in the world engage in foolish talk about how barbaric and unprincipled this would be. Their talk about the superiority of Western civilization is in the same category. In the West too only the scholars, a bunch of emptyheaded theorists, call for an end to war and aggression. Politicians and businessmen are not so impractical. To strengthen Japan by war is to show loyalty to our country and to our sovereign. That should be our guiding principle.[1]

At about the same time strategists at the War College were lecturing that Korea

[1] Quoted in Somura Yasunobu, "Tairiku seisaku ni okeru imēji no tenkai—Fukuzawa Yukichi no kōkeisha to tairukuha no hitobito" (Changing Images in Continental Policy—Fukuzawa Yukichi's Successors and the Continentalists), in *Kindai Nihon no seiji shidō* (Political Leadership in Modern Japan), eds. Shinohara Hajime and Mitani Taichirō (Tokyo, 1965), pp. 256–257.

was a dagger pointed at the heart of Japan and no third power should be allowed to possess it. The logic of this precept led next to the demand that land adjacent to Korea be taken over, and then still more land which could supply the resources necessary to make the home islands self-sufficient. The question naturally arises whether this conception of security was realistic or served Japan's interests very well.

Similar arguments were revived a few years ago. In several articles written in 1963–64, Hayashi Fusao, a novelist and journalist turned popular historian, proposed his thesis of "the hundred years war" to justify Japanese expansion and reinvigorate nationalism. From approximately the time of Perry's arrival until the 1940's, he contends, Japan was engaged in a series of related maneuvers and wars first to protect itself from Western imperialism, and then, as it grew stronger, to deliver all of East Asia from the white master. Japan expanded as a natural consequence of its quest for autonomy, and today the Japanese should cease apologizing for the Greater East Asia War since it marked the culmination of their defense of Asia against the West. The degree to which such notions were shared by those who advised the government or actually made the decisions on foreign policy in the earlier Meiji era is one of the major points at issue in this volume.

Skeptics protest that intervention and aggression are only made to seem rational, understandable, even justifiable when discussed in terms of security. If all countries have a natural right to the enjoyment of national sovereignty, then on what basis can country A convert country B into a satellite, buffer, or protectorate? How far outside its own borders should defense needs take a country? In Japan's case, the critics discern an impulse or urge to overseas expansion which existed quite apart from the legitimate requirements of security. Protection of national interests did not dictate the annexation of Korea or its subsequent harsh treatment. Japan was not the defender of Asia but its despoiler, along with the white man. Even more

bitter critics ask if Japan was not a little too alert to the important chances, a little too ready to take advantage of opportunities. Did Japan not in fact operate in accordance with a grand plan to conquer Asia dating back to the late 1860's? Stated in the bluntest way, Tokugawa aspirations became Meiji policies; and the Meiji Emperor and his advisers willed the continued expansion of Japan as their legacy to twentieth-century statesmen. Japan's expansion was scheming, systematic, ruthless, and premeditated. The aims of businessmen, politicians, and generals coalesced. One could never argue that Japan acquired an empire in a fit of absentmindedness, as did Britain at one point, or attribute Japanese behavior to the same kind of spontaneous outburst of energies, restlessness, and curiosity displayed by European peoples in the age of discovery, or compare Japan's actions with the supposedly well-intentioned but bumbling, hesitant expansionism of the United States.

Although conspiracy theories are common today as explanations for race riots, protest marches, the cold war, and political assassinations, the above charges may seem exaggerated. Those who know Japanese imperialism only as a chapter in a history book may find it hard to realize how often and with what conviction the Japanese have been accused of plotting to take over Asia. In large part, this is a result of projecting assumptions about Japanese leaders of the 1930's back into Meiji politics, a particularly dangerous practice if one at the outset is none too sure about the rationale of the 1930's. The past century is then viewed as a unified whole characterized by consistency of intention. This image of a diabolic Japan owes much to the wide publicity given in the 1930's to a document called the Tanaka Memorial, a plan for conquest supposedly presented by Prime Minister Tanaka Giichi to the emperor after a thorough review of Japan's China policy by high ranking civilian and military officials at a special Eastern Conference convened in Tokyo during June and July of 1927. The document first appeared in print in 1929 in an Eng-

lish language paper published on the
China coast; it is now considered very
probably a forgery. Yet the document
survives today in history texts and
sourcebooks as either the Japanese counterpart of Hitler's *Mein Kampf*—an open
declaration of intentions—or a valuable
clue to the views of influential Japanese,
since Japan subsequently behaved as
though it in fact had such a plan. One
widely used reader on imperialism contains among its approximately one hundred and eighty selections only two documents pertaining to Japan. One of them
is the Tanaka Memorial, bearing the label "Japan's Blueprint for Colonization
of the Far East, 1927."[2] It is also included in a recently published reader on
republican China under the title "The
Grand Plan for Conquest." Although the
editors do point out that the authenticity
of the documents is in question, they add
that this is irrelevant.[3] A lesser known
document of the same genre, first
brought to the attention of the world in
1905 and discussed in one of the selections of this book as the Kodama Plan of
1902, has been used to support a similar
plot thesis.

Hollywood made its contribution to
this image with a 1945 film, *Blood on
the Sun,* the stirring tale of fighting
newspaperman James Cagney's heroic
and nearly fatal struggle, assisted by the
Eurasian double agent Sylvia Sidney, to
smuggle proof of Japan's plan for conquest out of Tokyo in 1929. A certain
sinister Colonel Tōjō (Tōjō Hideki, later
chief of staff of the Kwantung Army in
Manchuria and prime minister from
1941–44, but at that time a section chief
in the bureau of supplies and equipment
of the War Ministry) is depicted as the
master mind in Baron Tanaka's cabinet
who draws up the memorial. He then
kills a brave cabinet liberal, Prince Tat-

sui (Hollywood's invention), who had
secretly attested to the authenticity of
the document in Cagney's presence but
first explained that he was doing this for
Japan's sake and not for the United
States. He would rather see Japan defeated than triumphant under the heels
of its militarists. When last seen, Cagney had escaped with the evidence, but
would the world believe him? A Hollywood fantasy, understandable at the end
of the war, but the taint lingers on, at
least on late night television. Unless the
authenticity of the document is considered a relevant question, what actually
happened at the Eastern Conference will
be ignored; and assessments of Japanese
foreign policy will be distorted, for the
memorial has been used to explain not
only Japan's subsequent behavior but
also its earlier expansion.

As several writers have already
pointed out, even if one were to assume
that the Japanese were more calculating
or efficient than other imperialists,
whether in the Meiji period or later,
there are many problems in proving a
conspiracy. It would be necessary to
postulate that the rulers and interest
groups in Japan possessed common motives and goals over the course of three
generations, that they were driven by the
same forces, had full control over a mal-
leable people, possessed the knowledge
and ability to manufacture incidents at
will while manipulating outsiders, and
that the world to which they responded
underwent very little change. Insistence
on the plot thesis may tell us more about
Japan's critics than about the Japanese
—what they wish to believe about Japanese national character and how they
prefer to explain complicated events.

Equally controversial is the counter-
argument that men do not and can not
dominate events. Individuals, it is said,
do not have much power in the shaping
of foreign policy. The Japanese statesmen, far from being villianous plotters,
were instead victims of unexpected
events or bureaucratic morass which
wrecked their cautious, reasoned approach to foreign relations. They are
seen as trapped by ignorance and chance
rather than driven by inherent evil. This

[2] The other is Foreign Minister Arita Hachirō
on "The Greater East Asia Co-Prosperity
Sphere, 1940." There is nothing on the earlier
period. See Louis Snyder, *The Imperialism
Reader, Documents and Readings on Modern
Expansionism* (Princeton: D. Van Nostrand
Co., 1962), pp. 93–97.
[3] Franz Schurmann and Orville Schell, eds.,
*Republican China, Nationalism War, and the
Rise of Communism, 1911–1949* (New York:
Vintage Books, 1967), pp. 178–185.

emphasis reflects a bias against conspiracy theories or paranoid interpretations of history. More to the point, it is also a result of failure to find tangible evidence of plots. In a more positive vein, it also expresses a different view about the nature of historical change. Nevertheless, the unconvinced have retorted that unexpected events often catalyze attitudes or bring latent ambitions to the surface. And, of course, what shapes the events or the men who react, or overact to them? The same statesman may at one time perceive himself to be the master of events and at another time their captive—or he may simply wait for events to make up his mind. Decisions are reactions to one thing and calculations about something else. "The fault, dear Brutus, is not in our stars but in ourselves," may be not only a good line in a Shakespearian play but also a fair guide to the facts of history.

There is still a third approach, as yet not very carefully worked out by historians of modern Japanese expansionism. One could try to show continuity of policy or general orientation and desire, as has been done by a new generation of historians in reinterpreting American foreign policy, without insisting upon the existence of conspiracies or plots. It would then become necessary to substantiate very carefully such claims as Japan's legacy of militarism or the expansionist nature of its political and economic institutions.

Another large question which troubles students of Japanese imperialism is the proper understanding and application to Japan of the concept of modernization. Included in this is the problem of analyzing the nature and significance of the Meiji Restoration of 1868. When one looks at the past century as a whole, were Japan's achievements a success or a failure? If we take 1840 or 1850 as a baseline, and even if we concede that Japan began its modern career at a high point, Japan's record by 1900 seems remarkable and equally so the rapidity of its recovery after 1945. Surely, Japan's record deserves study, even emulation, by the countries of Latin America, Asia, and Africa today although the circumstances of modernization have drastically changed. Then we remember the expansion, the ultranationalism, and the wars. How much were they a part of the "success"? Were they a necessary price to pay? Professor Ronald Dore contends that "the cost of Japan's foreign wars in human lives and resources was not incidental to Japan's development but an integral part of it. Aggressive nationalism and an expansionist foreign policy helped maintain internal unity, which enabled the state to mobilize resources for industrial development and even conditioned the disciplined acceptance of postwar reforms." Thus Japan's success and modern development were at the cost of the "lives and property" of other Asians and Americans as well as of Japanese.[4] This may be so, but again how much of this is unique to Japan's experience? What were the costs of American and European successes? One influential view of modernization points out that industrial societies may be created by either liberal or authoritarian means. Japan took the second road. Another argument is that truly modern societies are free, open, just, and affluent, whether capitalist or socialist in their basic organization. By this high standard, the United States is close but not yet fully modernized. And Japan's case then, before World War II, represents a perversion of the modernization process. Japan, a half-primitive, half-sophisticated society in the 1850's, in order to defend itself in a threatening world, was forced to engage in rapid modernization with no time for indulging in a liberal stage. The failure or inability of the Meiji leaders, who presided over the initial and crucial phases of this change, to allow a complete social revolution in the 1870's and 1880's, no matter how violent it would have been, produced the politics of oppression at home and aggression abroad. In short, for Commodore Perry to open Japan was to set in motion a chain of events leading inevitably to the invasion of China and the surprise attack on Pearl Harbor less

[4] "Latin America and Japan Compared," in *Continuity and Change in Latin America*, ed. John J. Johnson (Stanford, 1964), p. 234.

than a century later. For the sake of reflection and comparison, one could at this point refocus the lens and ask whether American society was such that its early Canton trade and the demands of Commodore Perry led inevitably to the clash with Japan, estrangement from China, and then involvement in Southeast Asia.

Revisionist scholars, many of whom were children during World War II, have been trying in recent years to test unproved assumptions about Japan, to pose new questions, and to track down new evidence now that the passions of war have cooled. Most of their work has been on the 1930's, but the earlier period has also received some attention. They have reassessed the character of the Sino-Japanese and Russo-Japanese wars, for example, in much the same way that American historians continually reappraise the Spanish-American war and its aftermath. They do not ascribe guilt or monstrous motives to Japan. They do not see blueprints for conquest in every government filing cabinet or interpret contingency plans as proof of plots. They ask if Japan began with limited objectives which then proved difficult to control. They are skeptical of Marxist formulas. Their efforts have earned them accusations of whitewashing the past or excusing the excesses of Japanese behavior. They reply that they do not wish to vindicate Japan but rather to learn how decisions were made and what motivated them, how attitudes and events shaped policies, and how behavior was related to class and occupation. Each case, they say, must be judged by its circumstances; each decision must be viewed in terms of the available options. If there must be judgments or condemnation, then let them be fair, for in the early period at least Japan, as a member of the club of gentlemen powers, was playing the imperialist game by Western standards. If scholars can agree that the explanation of Western imperialism is complicated, demanding a sophisticated assessment of evidence, then why not grant the same to Japan's experience.

These are the major, even extreme, formulations of the problem, and the selections which follow will reflect this range of questions and assumptions. In the prologue, a noted Japanese historian stresses the necessity of defense against the West—for a nation exists only if it retains its independence—without absolving Japan of responsibility for its decisions. The first section then compares the charge that imperialism was a perpetuation into modern times of a long history of expansionism with the rejoinder that it was a modern phenomenon—a response to the world of the late nineteenth century and having very little to do with the past, particularly the recent Tokugawa past which was isolationist. In the second section, the Meiji diplomatic and military establishments are examined, for, in the view of Meiji statesmen, both were necessary to Japan's defense. Here the argument centers on Japan's understanding of the world and international society, its conception of international law, and its application of the strategic axioms of modern military thought. Nationalism—and by extension, Pan-Asianism—is the theme of the third section. Just as Japanese imperialism is often portrayed as unusually malevolent, so is Japanese nationalism considered more hysterical and irrational than the patriotic sentiment of other people. Yet Japan's lingering pride in its Asian past and genuine sympathy for Asian aspirations—along with its successes in nation-building—won it a large following as the natural leader against Western imperialism. The various economic arguments, including the Marxist-Leninist analysis of the roots of Japanese aggression, will be found in the fourth section. The final section takes up the plot thesis and its rebuttal.

The defenders and opponents of these arguments still have a heavy burden of providing proof. Many conclusions have been based on research in only one language or one country's archives, and other problems have scarcely been touched. The relationship between Tokugawa aspirations and early Meiji expansionism has been only vaguely defined. Little has been written about the rise of aggressive ideologies or varieties of Pan-Asianism in Meiji Japan. There are few detailed studies, in Japanese or English, of the Sino-Japanese and Russo-Japanese wars. Japan's official and private dealings with various regions in East Asia and the Pacific—China, Manchuria, Mongolia, Siberia, Indo-China, Indonesia, the Philippines, Burma, Thailand, the islands of the South Seas, Australia, New Zealand, and Hawaii—are imperfectly understood. Much has been said about the indoctrination of Japanese schoolchildren with nationalist mythologies and religious awe for the emperor, but to what extent did this occur in the Meiji period? Why is an emperor-centered nationalism more aggressive than American manifest destiny, France's civilizing mission, or Victorian England's assumption of the white man's burden? Should the Tokugawa legacy to Meiji Japan be equated with militarism and political absolutism? What precludes military men from exercising progressive and responsible leadership? More needs to be known about Japanese anti-imperialism, including the criticisms of socialists, Christians, and liberal nationalists. Much has been suspected but little proved about the connections between continental adventurers and military intelligence, business circles, and politicians. How did the Japanese administer their various colonies, and did their techniques of control vary from place to place and time to time? Even if we can now see that empire building is in the long run unprofitable, on what assumptions did Japanese businessmen actually operate? These are only some of the questions which should be kept in mind in reading and judging the following selections.

NOTE: The Japanese name order has been followed in the selections, table of contents, and suggestions for additional reading: family name first and personal name last. In a few cases where there might be misunderstanding —that of Japanese-Americans or Japanese who reverse their name order to write in English— the family name has been capitalized. The macron or horizontal mark over certain vowels, an indication that the sound is prolonged, has been supplied in the translations and whenever the authors included them in the original publications. Most of the footnotes have been deleted, and all titles of the selections are the responsibility of the editor.

THE CONFLICT OF OPINION

Behind . . . Japanese hopes of social, economic, and political salvation, to be gained by territorial acquisition, lies a long history of dreams which seem to bear little relationship to population pressure, the need of markets and raw materials, political necessities, or strategic needs. . . . The history of Japanese expansion suggests . . . that the Japanese had no need to follow the bad examples of the empire builders of nineteenth century Europe. Indeed, the plea that the imitative and realistic Nipponese have, since 1871, merely copied the technique of the imperialistic white world, while plausible, is at times just faintly amusing.

——ROBERT T. POLLARD

. . . Japan was a latecomer to the contest for overseas empire. . . . Whatever experience Japan had known in overseas expansion and settlement lay, moreover, in so remote a past as to be more an historical memory than colonial tradition. . . .

In the same way that Shogunal policy after the conclusion of the Perry Treaty emanated from apprehension over western aggression, so too the foreign policy of the new government of the Meiji Emperor, established in 1868, was to a large extent founded on fear. The vigor of its activities notwithstanding, the Meiji regime was for long to be on the defensive in its international relations, its practical objectives being the maintenance of peace, the observation but ultimate abolition of the so-called "unequal treaties," and a modest expansion aimed at the promotion of the national security.

——HYMAN KUBLIN

. . . [Japan's] wars were not wars of defense, although they were treated as such in Japanese propaganda. They were wars of aggression. . . . They were the logical expression in foreign affairs of the ideas of the authoritarian state. They were the extension beyond Japan's borders of the militarism that had so long been characteristic of Japan.

——JOHN MAKI

If, as Clausewitz declared, war is the furtherance of diplomatic objectives by forceful means, one cannot escape the conclusion that Japan's handling of the Korean and South Manchurian problem during her conflicts with China and Russia mirrored a brilliant coordination of diplomacy and force under astute political leadership. Indeed, throughout the 1853–1910 period, Japan's military policies were invariably distinguished by the primacy of political leadership and political considerations, most noticeably in the clusters of decisions and reforms associated with the demise of the "closed door" and with the quest for an empire within the rules sanctioned by the diplomacy of imperialism.

——JAMES CROWLEY

The Genyosha and Kokuryukai . . . and their numerous offshoots have been . . . the advance guard of Japanese imperialism and have even thrust themselves into the position of an uninvited pilot who at times of great danger or uncertainty has played a decisive role in guiding Japanese policy along that charted course. It is these societies rather than any political party or succession of parties which have moulded public opinion in favor of aggression. They have provided continuity from one stage to the other in the unfolding strategy of Japanese expansionism.

——E. HERBERT NORMAN

. . . [T]o use the Confucian patterns and precepts for ruling and at the same time deny them as a guide for rulers, to reject the theory that a ruler governs under Heaven's mandate only so long as he is virtuous, made any revived Far Eastern order of the Japanese a mere facade for the exploitation of the neighboring peoples.

——M. FREDERICK NELSON

. . . [I]t is evident that during the Meiji Period ideas and ideals of Asiatic cooperation were more than the contrivance of Japanese imagination. They represented a reasonable and probable solution to a very present problem, and they were abandoned only gradually and reluctantly as the Chinese revolutionaries saw Japan try to justify a rule of Might with Oriental maxims of Right.

——MARIUS JANSEN

To the militarist fervor of the Japanese generals the bourgeoisie added its readiness for conquest as a means of increasing the rate of primitive capatalist accumulation, which was hindered by the small capacity of the internal markets of Japan. . . . [A]fter the ten-year period which lay between the Japanese-Chinese war and the Russo-Japanese war, Japanese capital speedily began to take on a new form and entered the new, imperialist, stage of its development.

——O. TANIN AND E. YOHAN

. . . the conclusion is clear and unequivocal: economic factors were negligible, insufficient, and unimportant. The Sino-Japanese War, though it was Japan's first big step toward annexation of Korea, was not an economic war, caused neither by Sino-Japanese trade rivalry in Korea nor by the penetration of the peninsula by Japanese capitalism.

——HILARY CONROY

One could go back through one hundred and fifty years noting Japanese programs for conquest, some set forth by private individuals and some proposed by responsible members of Government. . . . Japanese policy since 1868 has shown a singular consistency and uniformity, an undeviating purposefulness, that has been objective, cold, and calculating to a degree unconceivable in American thinking.

——GEORGE KERR

. . . premeditated murder and accidental death are very different things in courts of law, though the difference may be academic to the dead man. And it would seem to be of some consequence in working toward an understanding of the motive forces in international relations, as well as toward a fair appraisal of the Meiji government, to know whether they schemed the seizure of Korea, or were pushed into it by forces beyond their control, or fell into it through lack of foresight; whether honorable intentions turned dishonorable through ineptness, or whether they were dishonorable to begin with. And by what standard to measure them?

——HILARY CONROY

PROLOGUE

Oka Yoshitake

The opening words here are the work of Oka Yoshitake (1902–   ), Professor Emeritus of the Faculty of Law, University of Tokyo, a prolific writer on modern Japanese political and diplomatic history and one of Japan's most prominent scholars. In the following excerpts from an essay written in 1961, Professor Oka outlines the major themes in Japan's foreign relations from the end of the era of seclusion to the Russo-Japanese war. Many of the issues he touches upon will be examined in greater detail in other selections, but the great value of his work is his presentation of the problem from the perspective of a Japanese scholar. Throughout his largely factual summary, based on a selection of passages from official documents and polemical literature, Professor Oka injects his own view by consistently repeating the phrase *seiryoku tōzen*, the eastern advance of western power. This dramatically underlines his major point that fear of Western intentions in Asia was the chief element in shaping Japanese foreign policy. Western imperialism literally forced upon Japan a profound concern for national security. He does not, however, explain why Japan should feel more threatened than other Asian countries. He admits there was a previous record of expansionist sentiment but views Meiji overseas ventures as primarily the product of a new international environment. Japan's leaders were increasingly convinced that if Japan were to behave like a great power, and engage in empire building, there was less chance the West would interfere in their affairs or make insulting demands. At one point, there was much support both in and out of the government for cooperation of some sort with China and Korea to fend off the West. It collapsed, however, as the belief grew that China was doomed to remain corrupt and backward. So Japan was compelled to side with the West. One of the delusions, then, of modern Japan's foreign policy was the egocentric conviction that it could be strong at the expense of China.

A. "THE EASTERN ADVANCE OF WESTERN POWER" AND JAPAN'S SENSE OF NATIONAL CRISIS

1. The Meiji Restoration and National Independence

It is well known that in the final years of the Tokugawa shogunate, the steady progress in Asia of the "eastern advance of western power" thoroughly alarmed Japan's ruling military class and aroused a profound sense of danger to the nation's independence. From this was born the *sonnō-jōi* movement [revere the emperor and repel the barbarian], which turned on the question of whether or not to open Japan to friendship with the various great civilized countries of the West and convulsed the world of the shogunate. We might say that in its most extreme form *sonnō-jōi* was in our history an expression of nationalism generated

From Oka Yoshitake, "Kokuminteki kokuritsu to kokkai risei" (National Independence and the Reason for the State's Existence), in *Kindai Nihon shisōshi kōza* (Studies in the Political Thought of Modern Japan), VIII (Tokyo: Chikuma Shobō, 1961), 11–15, 17–30, 32–46 (section headings are those in the original text). Reprinted by permission of the author and publisher. [Editor's translation. Some corrections have been made in dates, and other minor liberties have been taken.]

by foreign pressure. Moreover, our national consciousness crystallized at a time when legends about the founding of the country were being reformulated, in particular, the idea of Japan as a "chosen" or divine country.

This *sonnō-jōi* movement served as the ideological preparation for the Meiji Restoration. As may be inferred, the restoration had in part the character of a national revolution. Such revolutions have as their aim national independence or expansion and require corresponding changes in the national structure. It was therefore quite natural for the Meiji government, itself the product of a reform upheaval, to make the maintenance of national independence a major concern. We can find evidence of such sentiment, for example, in a letter from Minister of State Iwakura Tomomi (1825–1883) to Chief Minister Sanjō Sanetomi, May 3, 1877, at the time of the Satsuma Rebellion: "When I look at conditions in our country and consider the situation, I keep thinking what a momentous time this is. *Since the restoration, we have had to promote unprecedented reforms in order to confront foreign countries. Although we had no choice but to adopt such a course, our policies have conflicted with general opinion in several points"* (italics in this and later quotations added by the author).

The new Meiji government tried to promote broad public acceptance of the idea of the sacred country and as a corollary to encourage the concept of emperor worship. The motives for doing this were complicated, but we can say that the policy stemmed in part from the desire to establish an ideological foundation for national independence. The important point to make here is that the Meiji leaders resolved to protect at all costs the independence of the nation in the face of "the eastern advance of western power." Their horror at the thought of being forced to yield to foreign pressure helps explain the emphasis on the idea of "the chosen country" of the emperor in their counter offensive. This can be illustrated by a passage in the "Imperial Letter to Pacify the Multitude" of April 6, 1868: "We hereby make an oath with all the government officials and the many lords to continue the great task bequeathed to Us by Our ancestors. With no thought of the hardships or difficulties We must undergo, We will Ourselves take charge of the administration and pacify the multitude. We wish *to spread the national glory far beyond the seas* and make the country secure like the towering Mt. Fuji." Another illustration will be found in Iwakura Tomomi's opinions on diplomacy contained in a memorandum sent to Sanjō Sanetomi in the second month following the restoration. He lamented that the new government's policy of friendship with the various foreign countries was not yet fully understood by the general public. They would have to make greater efforts to enlighten the people. But, they must also make the public understand:

Although there was no alternative to establishing diplomatic relations with foreign countries, *we must keep in mind that foreign countries are the national enemies of our imperial land.* What is a national enemy? All countries strive for wealth and power by steadily developing their arts and technology. All try to become superior to the others. A against B, B against A and C. Everywhere it is the same. And so I say that all foreign countries are the national enemies of our imperial land.

The new policy of friendship did not therefore rest simply on a more international outlook. Within it was concealed Iwakura's idea that "foreign countries are the national enemies of our imperial land." Along with anxiety over the very existence of the "chosen country," dreams of expansion were lurking in the darkness.

2. *The Korean Problem . . .*

Given the Meiji government's emphasis on preservation of national independence, what sort of policy was adopted and how was it carried out? The debate in 1873 over whether or not to send an expedition to Korea revealed disagreement on the requirements of security. Saigō Takamori (1827–77),

after his defeat in the debate and retreat to Satsuma, was quoted as admit-
ting that an attack by Japan on Korea
would probably provoke war with Russia. However, "Japan now claims Hokkaido. Can Japan stand up to Russia
with only Hokkaido? We should settle
the Korean question and expand from
Possiet Bay to Nikolaievsk. We should
definitely advance into Korea and so
protect our own country." Also, Saigō's
friend, Kirino Toshiaki (1838–77), argued when he left the government: "If
we want to make our country equal to
other countries and independent in the
world, we must go overseas, fight, and
make conquests. When we are comparable in strength to Europe and America,
we will be able to take our proper place
among the nations of the world." And
he further said: "We should want to
expand the Japanese islands. We should
not just remain on the defensive. We
should advance overseas and make conquests. If we shrink back, we cannot
guard our country. . . . In order to protect ourselves, we should attack the
enemy now. *We should not be content
to keep only what we already have.*
Otherwise, how could we continue to
remain independent? This is why Saigō,
myself, and the others want to expand
overseas."

In this view, Japan would prove itself a "great country" by expansion.
Only by creating a balance of power
with various Western countries could
we preserve our independence. This way
of thinking was common to the conquer
Korea faction, but such notions did not
in fact originate with this group. We
can detect their source in the views of
certain scholars of the late Tokugawa
period who were acutely aware of "the
eastern advance of western power" and
gravely concerned for the country (for
example, Hayashi Shihei, Honda Toshiaki, Satō Nobuhiro, Hashimoto Sanai,
and Yoshida Shōin).

The argument of the conquer Korea
faction was also conceived in response
to foreign pressure, "the eastern advance
of western power," and was, in effect a
plan inspired by military views. Its characteristics were threefold. First, it was
frühimperialismus or early imperialism,
in the sense that it did not serve the demands of "capital." Second, although its
advocates understood in a general way
the problem of power in international
politics, they were extremely naïve in
believing that the extent of a country's
territory was an essential ingredient of
power. Third, these men were quite
impractical in their comprehension of
what could be accomplished. Their fan-
tasies reflected their heightened sense
of national crisis.

The Iwakura mission, which had
gone abroad to study Western countries
and prepare the way for treaty revision,
returned in 1873 and opposed the plans
of the conquer Korea faction, preventing
their realization. The anti-war faction
had come back from the foreign tour
deeply shocked by the difference between the level of civilization in Japan
and the countries of the West and therefore convinced that it was more urgent
to promote Japan's internal modernization than to risk danger abroad. . . .
This outcome should not obscure the
fact that there was no opposition to expansion itself, even within the anti-war
group. The real issues were concrete
measures and timing. Our proof is the
authorization of an expedition to Formosa the following year (1874) by a
government under the control of the
very same men who had opposed the
conquest of Korea. Nevertheless, the
main focus of government policy was
now domestic reform. In the meantime
the great trend of "the western advance
of eastern power" had not lost its mo-
mentum. The chief victim was China,
but western imperialism also made vigorous advances in Southeast Asia and
the South Pacific. The sole point of difference between this time and the last
days of the Tokugawa shogunate was
that Western pressure was not directly
applied to our country. . . .

3. *Traditional Arguments for Sino-Japanese Cooperation*

. . . Scholars of the late Tokugawa
era had already grasped the lesson that
Western imperialism in neighboring
China could spread and that it threat-

ened great danger to our national independence. This fact had not changed at all after the restoration. Instead of viewing China's fate under Western imperialism as simply a fire on the opposite shore, the Japanese quite naturally felt deep concern. And not only that, many felt even some sense of solidarity with China. It was frequently asserted that the two countries were in a "lips and teeth or wheel and axle" relationship [stereotyped phrases for mutual dependence]. Supporters of Sino-Japanese cooperation believed that together the two countries could defend their independence and resist the pressure of Western imperialism. Some even thought that Korea should eventually be added to form a sort of triple alliance.

. . . Negotiations in 1871 between China and Japan resulted in a treaty of friendship. We can see the direct influence of the argument for alliance in article two of the treaty: "Now that friendly relations exist between the two countries, this friendship shall, without fail, be of an intimate and reciprocal character. Should either State experience at the hands of another country injustice or insulting treatment, on communication being made to the other State the latter shall give assistance or use its good offices in mediating between the two countries. Thus friendship shall be increased." Iwakura Tomomi argued in a memorial to the emperor, February, 1875, that Russia was the country to fear most among the various foreign powers. If China were annexed by Russia, the independence of Japan would be endangered. For this reason Japan should try to be friendly with China, for by mutual assistance and cooperation both could ensure their "complete independence." Several years later, in October of 1882, a time of very tense relations between Japan and China caused by an ugly incident in Korea, Iwakura pointed out in a memorandum to Foreign Minister Inoue Kaoru that in Asia only China and Japan had managed to preserve their independence. If these two countries did not act together, it would be impossible ultimately to prevent "the eastern ad-

vance of western power." There were also ardent advocates of cooperation with China outside of the government, and many references to the argument can be found scattered throughout contemporary memorials and commentaries. . . .

It is especially important to note that this support for Sino-Japanese cooperation rested upon two assumptions. First, Western imperialism in Asia had instilled great fear even in the popular mind, a point I have stated repeatedly. Second, Japan traditionally had a high estimate of China's power. Because of this, China was thought to have the proper qualifications (*bündnisfähig*) to be our ally.

4. *The Genesis of the Argument to Reconstruct China and Korea*

. . . In our country modernization was thought to be indispensable to maintain national independence. Since China was slow to adopt Western learning, even though it was under the direct pressure of Western imperialism, many Japanese became uneasy about China's ability to remain independent. This did not necessarily mean there was heartfelt sympathy for China's fate. Rather, it was believed that our security was directly related to theirs. For this reason, some Japanese who supported China's modernization efforts began to withdraw suggestions for cooperation. I think we may say that this change in sentiment was to be expected, given such conditions.

Fukuzawa Yukichi (1834–1901) boasted in his essay, "A Critique of the Times," 1881, that no country in the East could match Japan in the adoption of Western learning and progress in civilization. Whereas the Chinese were slow to attain enlightenment, the Japanese alone among the peoples of the East could stand with the West "at the center of civilization." Therefore, "we should resolve to make the protection of East Asia our responsibility." Some Japanese, he continued, believe that it is proper to take measures for their own independence, but useless to protect others. This is not so. For example, suppose we have a stone house. If there are wooden buildings in the neighborhood, we must still worry about fires. In fire prevention, we have to think about the whole neighborhood and not only our own house. If there is an emergency, we give aid, of course. But it is a serious matter to enter a neighbor's house on an ordinary day and demand that he reconstruct it with stone, like ours. The neighbor will do as he pleases and may or may not build a new house. In an unusual case, we might have to force our way in and build this house ourselves, not for the sake of the neighbor but to stop the fire from spreading. The way in which Western countries are now expanding their influence in Asia is analogous to the spreading of fire. Neighboring Korea and China, which have no equal in foolishness, are like wooden houses unable to survive a fire. So Japan must "give them military protection" and "be their cultural inspiration," not for their sake but for ours. If necessary, "we must threaten to use force if they don't make progress" and allow no opposition. "Although it is commonly said that we have a 'lips and teeth' relationship with them as between equals, to think that there could be any cooperation between us and China in its present state is the height of stupidity."

. . . Among those who advocated the reform of China, two groups deserve our attention. The first was the *freedom and popular rights movement,* which vigorously challenged the Satsuma-Chōshū clique government. It is well known that there were many violent objections to clique government in the period before the Sino-Japanese war, but the popular rights people were also very much concerned with the question of national independence. They reasoned that through democratization the people would come to shoulder the burden of national defense and identify with the fate of the nation. Thus the state would be even stronger in confronting the outside world. . . . This in turn prompted much discussion of the problem of Asia's regeneration. . . .

For example there was Sugita Teiichi (1851–1920), a member of the Jiyūto or Liberal Party, who published a "plan to revive Asia" in 1884. He argued that intellectual exchange was essential to reverse the decline of Asia and suggested that cooperative associations be organized. Later that year, when the Franco-Chinese war broke out, he went over to China, thinking he would try to set up schools for the training of able men and so help China resist the pressure of Western imperialism. Also he hoped to enlighten influential people both in and out of government, who would then work to strengthen China and, in imitation of Japan, establish a parliament. . . . He later explained in his reminiscences that he had gone to China in 1884 because the Meiji Emperor had already promised a parliament in Japan and the basis for constitutional government had been laid. "For the moment, this was no longer an issue in Japan, and it was now time to promote the *independence of Asia and the freedom of the East.* I thought we should begin by replanting the seeds of liberty and popular rights on the continent." . . .

Representative of the second group of reformers were Arao Kiyoshi (1859–96), Nezu Hajime (1860–1927), and their circle of associates. Arao and Nezu were both army men. Nezu had entered the Military Academy in 1879 and Arao a year later. This was a time of great infatuation with European fads, but these two students paid close attention to the activities of Russia within the general movement of "the eastern advance of western power." If the trend were to continue, the danger to Asia was obvious. They resolved to defend Asia against Western imperialism by promoting cooperation between China and Japan. Enlightenment would make China strong and prosperous. Neither was taken in by the currently fashionable but superficial adoration and imitation of Western culture. Arao went to China in 1886 and formed a trade company in Hankow which he named the Razukendō [The Hall of Pleasurable Delights]. In 1890, he founded the Sino-Japanese Trade and Research Institute in Shanghai. Nezu soon joined him, and the two men retired from active army duty to devote their efforts to such enterprises. They dreamed of enabling both countries to resist "the eastern advance of western power" and of making Sino-Japanese trade more prosperous. Close economic ties, they believed, would serve as the foundation for political collaboration. . . . They of course had more in mind than the promotion of trade. They wanted to encourage the reconstruction of China. When Russia announced its plans in 1887 to build a Trans-Siberian railway, Arao predicted that the result would be a sharp increase in the pressure of Western imperialism on China and Korea. Japan had only ten years in which to complete the reform of China. Arao worked hard toward this end, but did not live to see his hopes realized.

5. Growing Support for the Argument to Expand on the Continent

We must keep in mind that the relations between Japan and China were tense after the restoration despite the talk about Sino-Japanese cooperation to resist the "eastern advance of western power." The Taiwan expedition in 1874 and the Korean incident in 1884 were both for a time crises verging on war. Ten years after the 1884 incident, there was finally the sudden eruption of war between Japan and China. Thus by some strange coincidence the relations between the two countries met with crisis and then catastrophe in ten year cycles. With the exception of the Taiwan expedition, the main source of trouble was the Korean problem, in particular China's assertion of suzerainty over Korea. Without repeating the story, let me say simply that since the Korean peninsula was so close to us geographically, its domination by a third power was regarded as a great threat to our national independence. In the period up to the Sino-Japanese war, China was the country which troubled us most. Very early the Meiji government made the removal of Korea from China's influence one of its chief diplo-

matic aims. It refused, for example, to recognize China's claims to suzerainty when negotiating the 1876 treaty of friendship with Korea.

In such a chronically unstable and dangerous situation, it was inevitable that there would be a rebuttal to the argument for Sino-Japanese cooperation. Iwakura Tomomi, in the 1882 memorial to which I previously alluded, insisted that if Japan and China did not cooperate, Japan could not stop the "eastern advance of western power." To risk war with China over "petty" Korea would bring no benefit to Japan. We would simply fatten the purses of the cunning European merchants. . . .

. . . However, critics of this approach were unnerved by the continuing disruption in China and urged that Japan extend its authority to China and Korea. If the powers ever began to partition China, Japan must be sure to participate and share in the spoils. The assumption was that Japan, by joining, could tip the international balance of power in its favor and so maintain its independence. . . .

Let me try to illustrate these various points. I have already mentioned Sugita Teiichi's trip to China. According to his reminiscences, what he saw when he arrived "was decay truly beyond imagination and description." . . . In his Lingering Impressions from a Tour of China, 1884, he criticized the Chinese as "narrow-minded and obstinate; they do not know the great trends of the world." The Western countries were competing for profits in East Asia and scheming to obtain a dominant position. China was about to become a battleground of Western imperialism, with Japan as a spectator. Rather than being "meat," Japan should go ahead and become "a guest at the table." This was the "law of the survival of the fittest in the real world." Some might say that China was to Japan a "lips and teeth country" and so relations should be friendly, but how could we be intimate with the Chinese who so foolishly clung to old things? Not only that, they did not show in their diplomacy any friendship for our country. This was how

Sugita reassessed matters after seeing the actual situation in China. . . .

Fukuzawa, who had previously admitted that he was not opposed to using the threat of force to make China and Korea reform, now wrote in 1885 the essay, "On Shedding Asia," for his newspaper *Jiji Shimpō*. In today's world, he said, it was not possible to remain independent without introducing Western civilization. Therefore, Japan had adopted modern learning in all things and spurned old customs. It was acting in a new way in Asia. Fukuzawa described this behavior with the phrase, *datsu-A,* or "shedding Asia."[1] China and Korea, contrary to Japan, had closely guarded their traditions and so could not be expected to preserve their independence. It would be remarkable if they were to undergo changes like those inspired by our Meiji Restoration. But if they did not, they would become "ruined countries." There was not the slightest doubt that their territories would be divided up by the civilized countries of the world. They were supposed to be "lips and teeth" allies but China and Korea were not only useless but the civilized people of the West were apt to lump Japan in the same category as those two half-civilized countries. Because of this, Japan often met frustration in its conduct of diplomacy. Fukuzawa had a remedy:

We must not wait for neighboring countries to become civilized so that we can together promote Asia's revival. Rather we should leave their ranks and join forces with the civilized countries of the West. *We don't have to give China and Korea any special treatment just because they are neighboring countries.* We should deal with them as Western people do. Those who have bad friends cannot avoid having a bad reputation. I reject the idea that we must continue to associate with bad friends in East Asia.

[1] *Datsu-A* is often translated "escape from Asia," or "departure from Asia." *Datsu,* divorced from the compound *dasshutsu,* to get out of or escape, can also be read as the verb "to take off," "cast off," or "shed," and shedding Asia or the Asian identity seems to express Fukuzawa's meaning best. [Editor's note.]

. . . And so arguments like Fukuzawa's on "shedding Asia" or advancing onto the continent made their appearance. However, in the period up to the Sino-Japanese war the sentiment for cooperation with China (or China, Japan, and Korea) apparently remained as influential as before.

6. *The Sino-Japanese War and the Triple Intervention*

At the beginning of the Sino-Japanese war, our aim was to destroy the suzerain-vassal relationship between China and Korea . . . and to drive Chinese power from the peninsula in order to guarantee Japan's independence. It was thus a war with a very pronounced military and political character. . . . The lingering high estimate of China, however, made the Japanese people very nervous at the beginning. But when victories unexpectedly and rapidly piled up through our overwhelming military superiority, feelings so changed that, to quote from the diary of our foreign minister at that time, Mutsu Munemitsu (1844–1897), "the people, who before the news of Heijō and the Yellow Sea were privately very anxious about the final outcome, now have no doubt of an early victory. It is only a question of time before the flag of the rising sun advances to the doors of Peking. The spirit of the country soars to heights of ecstasy. Everywhere the people are overflowing with pride and arrogance, and intoxicated with songs and cries of victory." . . . In this heady atmosphere, various sanguinary visions were spawned of the future when Japan would pile up magnificent victory upon magnificent victory. For example, Yamagata Aritomo (1838–1922), who had been one of the pro-war group within the government, went off to the front as the chief military commander. In a memorial which he sent to the emperor from the battlefield, he recommended that Japan construct a railroad from Pusan and Seoul to Ŭiju [a town near the mouth of the Yalu River]. "The Pusan-Ŭiju railroad will be a great road. I have no doubt that in the future it will pass through China and reach India. If our country wishes to assume leadership in Asia and gain lasting ascendency among the great powers, I am convinced we must extend this road straight to India."

If we shift our attention to the political parties . . . , we will find similar views, as in the September 19, 1894 issue of the Liberal Party newsletter. Its prediction was that war would soon break out in Europe and "Western institutions and culture would crumble and collapse." . . . The European powers had made blunders in colonization and would be forced to retreat. As they began to decline at the beginning of the twentieth century, "Japan would tower aloft at one end of East Asia and soar above the myriad nations of the world." Also Ozaki Yukio (1858–1954), who was then a leader of the Kaishintō (Progressive Party), said in one of his speeches that Japan, in order to obstruct "the eastern advance of western power" after the war, should conquer China and place it under the rule of the emperor. . . .

*   *   *

. . . The war intensified the menace of Western imperialism, and Japan was very much aware of this. Fukuzawa warned that as a result of China's loss of dignity at home and abroad civil war was likely to break out within a few years and so encourage partition by the Western imperialist powers. Japan "could observe this happening from its position in the East and in case of dismemberment had the power to get a valuable place in China in a strategic spot." He wanted Japan to anticipate Europe and be sure to get territorial concessions at the end of war, that is "a base of operations adequate for the expansion of power into the field of contest" once the partition began (*Jiji Shimpō*, December 13, 1894). . . .

. . . In 1895 at the Shimonoseki peace conference, Japan's demands included the cession of the Liaotung peninsula to prevent China from making inroads again in Korea and also a huge indemnity of 200,000,000 taels, apparently to hamper China's economic recovery.

The request that three additional cities be opened to Japanese trade, residence, and industry was an attempt to counter Western opposition by offering a share in the benefits of the war; for through the most favored nation clauses of the unequal treaties, whatever Japan gained the powers would automatically gain. It is probably not necessary to add here that the demand for the cession of Liaotung and Taiwan was linked with the will to expand. At Shimonoseki, our country forced China to agree to a new treaty of commerce and navigation modeled upon the commercial treaties between China and the West. For a long time after the restoration Japan had agonized over its own treaty revision problem; now it stood in a privileged position similar to the West's by concluding an unequal treaty with China. And so it was that on the occasion of its victory in the Sino-Japanese war, Japan took the first great step along the road suggested by Fukuzawa's "shedding Asia."

Unfortunately, soon after the treaty was signed, Japan was confronted by the triple intervention (Russia, France, and Germany), with the result that it was forced to give up the Liaotung peninsula. The triple intervention was truly a profound shock. Although the public was told repeatedly during the war to be prepared for a future offensive of Western imperialism, such pressure had materialized rather suddenly. Although Japan had won a glorious victory, it was made painfully conscious of how little weight it carried in East Asian international power politics. Kuga Katsunan (1857–1907) warned in commenting upon Japan's acquiescence to the retrocession that "international matters should sometimes be handled by force; we cannot contest them by reason alone" (*Nihon*, May 27, 1895). . . . S. L. Gulick wrote in his book, *The White Peril in the Far East* (1905) that through the recent negotiations for treaty revision "Japan discovered that European diplomacy was not based on right, but on private interests and especially on might. Japan had expected to secure her rights from Europe by qualifying for them.

She discovered in the early nineties that Europe had no interest in her rights and would not respect them until forced to do so by Japan's might." There is no doubt that the bitter experience of the triple intervention, along with the treaty revision issue, made our people even more painfully aware of their low international stature while simultaneously reinforcing the tendency in the country to rely on power politics in international relations. . . .

B. THE AGE OF "SHEDDING ASIA"

1. Popular Sentiment and the Anglo-Japanese Alliance

. . . After the war Japan's leaders authorized a program of armaments expansion and cast Russia in the role of hypothetical enemy. They were alarmed at Russia's imperialist activities in Korea and sincerely wished to maintain "China's integrity" and prevent partition. Confronted by this, some Japanese continued to favor Sino-Japanese cooperation. In 1898, for example, the Tōa Dōbunkai [East Asian Common Culture Society] was organized by Inukai Tsuyoshi (1855–1932) and Konoe Atsumaro (1863–1904), and in 1901 it set up the East Asian Academy in Shanghai, with Nezu Hajime as the director. The "Prospectus" of the society emphasized the antiquity of relations between China, Japan, and Korea. The three were like "brothers" by virtue of a common culture and ethics. Recent hostilities among them, however, had given Western countries a chance to intervene, and the situation had become grave. Therefore, the "governments," "businessmen," and "military leaders" of the three countries should be friendly and cooperate in order to make all of them prosperous and strong. Also, the Shanghai Academy, according to its "Statement of Purpose," was set up: "to give lectures in China and elsewhere on practical knowledge, to teach talented Chinese and Japanese and thereby establish the foundation for China's wealth and strength, to make a firm foundation for mutual cooperation between China and Japan, to make the whole nation of China secure and so promote lasting peace in East Asia and ensure eternal peace in the world." . . .

Among the Japanese who supported cooperation with China after the 1894–95 war were the China *rōnin* or adventurers. They were all interested in the continent but had diverse political motives. The *rōnin* of such ultra-nationalist societies as the *Genyōsha* (Dark Ocean Society) and *Kokūryukai* (Black Dragon Society), Tōyama Mitsuru (1855–1944) and Uchida Ryōhei (1874–1939), for example, wanted to expand Japanese influence in China through contacts with revolutionary factions. But others were more altruistic, like Miyazaki Torazō (1870–1922) and Hirayama Shū (1870–1949), who were very close to Sun Yat-sen (1866–1925) and gave generously of themselves to revolutionary projects for the reconstruction of China. Then in 1899, the Boxer Uprising suddenly began. This was in essence resistance to Western imperialism by the yellow race as the Chinese people now rose up to oppose the partition of China. Our country sent troops to north China in a joint expedition with the Western imperialist countries and helped suppress the Boxers. In 1895 we had acquired through the unequal peace treaty imposed on China a position of equality with the Western powers in dealing with that country. This time we went further and sought to dampen, in cooperation with the Western powers, the explosion of nationalism which had erupted among the Chinese people. Thus, Japan took another step forward in the direction of "shedding Asia."

During the Boxer incident, Russian troops occupied Manchuria and were in a position to put pressure on Korea. Our country, which had been watching the movement of Russian imperialism in Korea ever since the Sino-Japanese war, interpreted this move as a grave threat to Japan's security. To cope with the problem, the government concluded the Anglo-Japanese Alliance in January, 1902, hoping to restrain the Russians and reduce the possibility of war. The general public was very enthusiastic about the alliance, as is apparent from comments in leading newspapers and journals. . . . Why was the public so pleased? For one reason, the prospect of partnership with a great world power like Britain made the Russian menace in Manchuria less frightening. . . . This great satisfaction, however, was also closely related to our national inferiority complex about Japan's international status. This had worsened after the shock of the triple intervention. An editorial in the *Jiji Shimpō* expressed very well the relief now felt throughout Japan upon being liberated from such anxiety. "It seems almost like an impossible dream when we consider how exalted Japan has become only forty years after opening the country to the rest of the world and just five or six years after demonstrating our strength for the first time in the Sino-Japanese war. Our country has now become, both in name and reality, one of the world powers" (February 14, 1902). . . .

2. Tension in our Relations with Russia

The Anglo-Japanese Alliance, however, was not effective in checking Russian imperialism in Manchuria. Furthermore, Russia was also attempting to put pressure on Korea. Our government proposed a diplomatic solution to this crisis through the policy of *Man-Kan kōkan*, exchanging Manchuria for Korea, but the negotiations faltered and agreement seemed remote. In this situation, there was increasing public support for a war with Russia and much criticism of the offer of Korea for Manchuria. . . . There were two basic arguments against giving up Manchuria. First, if Manchuria were placed under Russian control, the independence of adjacent Korea could not long be maintained and in consequence Japan's security would also be jeopardized. Second, Manchuria had value as a market and an outlet for excess population. For example, an editorial in the *Nihonjin* (October 20, 1903) stressed the importance of Manchuria to Japan and advocated going to war with Russia immediately. In the event of victory, Japan should annex Manchuria, or if this proved impossible make it a protector-

ate, since in this modern age of "imperialism" it was exceedingly difficult for a small country to preserve its independence.

Very few had the courage to voice anti-war sentiment in a Japan now thoroughly aroused by arguments in favor of war. One of them was General Tani Tateki (1837–1911), who during the Sino-Japanese war had urged a generous peace settlement with China. . . . In 1903, he was insisting that the problem of Russian troop withdrawals from Manchuria should be settled between Russia and China. There was no justification for Japan's going to war with Russia over this issue. The people and the intellectuals who wanted to kick Russia out of Manchuria by military force also spoke of turning Manchuria into a Japanese colony. They were wrong to be sanguine about Japan's chances in a war with Russia. Tani harshly criticized the widespread opinion in favor of war as "foolish from a military point of view, and arrogant, rude, and in total violation of the rules of international behavior" (February 25, 1903). . . . However, such convictions were very rare in those days. . . .

3. Coping with the Fear of a Yellow Peril

In the period just before the Russo-Japanese war there was also pronounced public concern in Japan about charges of a "yellow peril." Ever since Kaiser William II coined the phrase, after the demonstration of our military strength to the world in the Sino-Japanese war, suspicions like this were frequently expressed in Europe. It was a sign of uncertainty in Western imperialist countries about the consequences of the rise of Japan for the future of colonialism in Asia. . . . For example, an article in the October 5, 1903 issue of *Nihonjin* declared that the world had come to fear us because of the opinion of certain experts that Japan would defeat Russia should there be a war. Surely the white race would dread this outcome as a serious blow to the prestige of "the Aryan race" and damaging to the power and confidence of the white man. Undoubtedly Russia would appeal to the racial prejudice of white people to strengthen its position against Japan. . . . On this point, Prime Minister Katsura Tarō's statement to the foreign representatives in Tokyo, May, 1904, after the war had begun is worthy of notice. He compared the war to the British and Russian rivalry in Persia and said Japan was motivated by a desire for security and the eternal peace of the East. He emphasized that this war was neither racial nor religious in character, that it had absolutely nothing to do with those things but was instead for justice, humanity, world trade, and civilization.

What was the source of this great anxiety in Japan over the charge of a yellow peril? Our diplomacy, as related above, was following the road of "shedding Asia." . . . Even though Japan was a part of Asia, we were trying to maintain or enlarge our colonial rule on the continent just like the Western imperialist countries. It therefore naturally followed that we would join the Western imperialist countries and either confront, compromise, or cooperate with them. The formation of a common anti-Japanese front by the Western imperialist countries under the influence of the yellow peril scare would isolate Japan, since we had already turned our back on Asian countries, and make it difficult either to advance or retreat. For us this would be not only an obstruction on the road of "shedding Asia" but also a threat to national independence. As a result of these worries, the yellow peril issue was treated with extreme caution. . . .

4. *The Russo-Japanese War and the Further Development of the Tendency to "Shed Asia"*

The Russo-Japanese war began in February, 1904. Japan was in a state of extreme tension since it was fighting a big European country. However, like the Sino-Japanese war, there was soon mounting national pride as Japan scored successive victories and the war went favorably for our side. After the ultimatum was delivered to Russia, the *Jiji Shimpō* stated that the actions of Japan were intended "to fulfill the *divine mission of spreading the light of civilization throughout the Eastern world*" (February 7, 1904). A few days later, this paper said that even though Russia was located in Europe and had the outward appearance of a civilized country, the people's way of thinking was not yet civilized. Our country would reveal to the world that Russia "was actually extremely barbarous behind its mask of civilization." . . . The *Nihon,* essentially a conservative and nationalist newspaper, took the same position and said in an editorial written just before the Portsmouth Peace Conference that Japan should be prepared to continue the war, for "the enemy is an uncivilized country which has not yet shed the traditions of the Mongols and which tries to disturb the peace of the civilized world. . . . At present, and for the sake of the civilized world, we have no choice but to continue the war until we have crushed their evil designs" (August 4, 1905).

The opinions I have cited are of considerable interest. Japan's pride in itself as a civilized nation, in contrast to backward Russia, corresponded with the process of "shedding Asia" and joining the ranks of the Western imperialist countries. It was a corollary of the belief that our country, unlike other Asian countries, belonged to the bloc of Western civilization. Also representative of this view was the argument of Ueda Mannen (1867–1939) in a talk published in 1904 that the Japanese should ignore those people in the West who voice ignorant opinions like the yellow peril and should have self-respect; for "even though we belong to the same yellow race, we Japanese are a civilized people and are not to be treated like the Chinese, Koreans, and other East Asians." . . .

The war ended with the Portsmouth Peace Treaty in September, 1905. It is well-known that the Japanese public was extremely disappointed in the lenient terms and resentful. They feared the treaty would not check Russian imperialist activities in Manchuria and Korea. . . . The victory, however, further aroused apprehension in Western imperialist countries about Japan's intentions, and the cries of "yellow peril" were heard once more. And our victory encouraged Asian nations which had been suffering for many years under the yoke of Western imperialism. By destroying "the myth of the invincibility of the white face," Japan seemed to be a great champion which was leading the fight against the rule of Western imperialism in Asia. There was reason now to hope for liberation.

Contrary to these expectations, our country started marching in the opposite direction after the Russo-Japanese war. By the Portsmouth Treaty we had already won Russia's acquiescence to our establishment of a protectorate over Korea; five years later we annexed that country. Also we began to exploit Manchuria after inheriting Russia's imperialist rights and interests in southern Manchuria. Later, in 1907, the Russo-Japanese Trade Agreement was concluded for the purpose of maintaining and strengthening each other's imperialist position in China in opposition to American imperialism. Our country also accepted the role of reinforcing British rule over India by negotiating the renewal of the Anglo-Japanese Alliance toward the end of the Russo-Japanese war. Finally, Japan promised in the Franco-Japanese Trade Agreement of 1907 to respect French control over Indo-China. By these treaties, Japan moved closer to the side of the Triple Entente powers and became increasingly entangled in the subtleties of world politics growing out of the antagonism between the Triple Entente and the Triple Alliance. And so our country advanced further along the road of "shedding Asia" and became deeply involved with the camp of the Western imperialist countries.

I. ANCIENT DREAMS AND PRESENT FEARS

Robert T. Pollard

TRADITIONAL EXPANSIONISM

Professor Pollard (1897–1939) began his teaching career as an instructor at St. John's University in Shanghai in 1923 and was at the time of his death executive officer of the Department of Oriental Studies, University of Washington. The following paper was first presented at the annual meeting of the American Historical Association, December, 1938. In it he charged that the Japanese had been an expansionist and aggressive people from the beginning of their recorded history. Therefore, it was natural for them to turn imperialist in the late nineteenth century because they had always been power-hungry and anxious to dominate Asia, if not the world. Pleas of self-defense and special economic needs were only pretexts and not the real causes of empire-building. Pollard's evidence ranges from militant passages in ancient Japanese chronicles and poems to the reality of Hideyoshi's invasions of Korea in the 1590's; it includes demands for empire in the chauvinistic literature written during the last hundred years of Tokugawa rule when Japan began to feel threatened first by Russian and then by British expansion. Among the dozens of prominent late Tokugawa writers, he emphasizes the martyred Yoshida Shōin (1830–1859), teacher of several of the Meiji statesmen and one of the most revered heroes in modern Japanese history and folklore. Pollard assumes that Yoshida perpetuated the ancient longings for empire through his students. Only circumstances delayed their realization until 1894. Pollard wrote his paper with Japan's invasion of China fresh in mind; but similar assumptions persist today in scholarly and popular treatments of Japan's early modern empire, although anti-Japanese passions have cooled and archives are open to more rigorous historical research. (Note that it is still debatable whether the Tokugawa polemics on security problems should be called expansionist, nationalist, or defense literature. There is as yet no comprehensive study of their contents, the motives of their authors, or their influence.)

B EHIND . . . [present-day] Japanese hopes of social, economic, and political salvation to be gained by territorial acquisition, lies a long history of dreams which seem to bear little relationship to population pressure, the need of markets and raw materials, political necessities, or strategic needs. There was a period in the development of mankind when territorial expansion did not have to be rationalized or justified. They took who had the power, and they held who could. The moral opinion of mankind was either nonexistent or of little consequence, and there was no public opinion toward which a calculating eye had to be cocked. It is only very recently that the Japanese themselves, having

From Robert T. Pollard, "Dynamics of Japanese Imperialism," *Pacific Historical Review*, VIII (March, 1939), pp. 16–18, 20–29.

taken on the sophistication of the modern world, have seen fit to offer explanations of or excuses for territory grabbing. The history of Japanese expansion suggests, incidentally, that the Japanese had no need to follow the bad examples of the empire builders of nineteenth century Europe. Indeed, the plea that the imitative and realistic Nipponese have, since 1871, merely copied the technique of the imperialistic white world, while plausible, is at times just faintly amusing.

There is, for instance, the sixteenth century scheme of the great Japanese captain, Toyotomi Hideyoshi, to conquer a continental empire of amazing dimensions. Having mastered and unified Japan as it had not been unified for two centuries, Hideyoshi looked abroad for new worlds to conquer. In 1590, he notified the King of Korea of his intention to proceed to the conquest of China, and demanded that the monarch coöperate with him in the ambitious enterprise. In his letter to the Korean King, Hideyoshi recalled that before his birth his mother had dreamed that the Sun—which in Japanese mythology has a very special significance—had entered her bosom. Interpreting this dream, a physiognomist had predicted that the child was destined to extend his authority "to all parts of the world wherever the sun shines," and that after he came to manhood his "benevolent rule would be admired by nations in every direction" and "people within the four seas" would all come under his influence and power. Already he had established complete control over the sixty-six provinces of Japan whose people waxed prosperous under his benevolent rule, and he now announced his intention—quite without reference to population statistics or the need for markets—of proceeding to the conquest of China, where the people were to be compelled "to adopt our customs and manners." The great conqueror ended his letter with the demand that the King of Korea become his military ally and coöperate with him in the destruction of the Ming dynasty. Subsequently it became apparent that Hideyoshi planned to induce

the Emperor of Japan to remove his capital from Kyoto to Peking, where he would be enthroned as the "Ruler of the Great Empire." Thus Korea was to be, not a dagger pointed at the heart of Japan, but a highroad over which Japanese troops marched to glory and victory on the continent. Letters which Hideyoshi wrote also to the King of Liuchiu [known to the Japanese as the Ryukyu Islands], the rulers of the Philippines and Formosa, and the ruler of India make it very clear that the dreams of conquest extended also to those territories. One goes back to Genghis Khan and the Mongols for anything comparable. Had Hideyoshi not died in 1598, six years after the beginning of the Korean invasion, it is not impossible that at least part of his great dream might have been realized.

In a sense, Hideyoshi, with his seemingly fantastic convictions of national and personal destiny, was merely the heir of a very ancient tradition in Japan. One of the oldest of Japanese historical chronicles is the *Nihongi* or *Nihonshoki* [Records of Japan], reduced to writing in the year 720 of our era. This chronicle, together with its companion work, the *Kojiki* [Record of Ancient Matters], completed in 712, serves not merely as a bible of the Shinto religion, but as a textbook as well for the Shinto school of historians. In these early records appear accounts of how the Sun Goddess, Amaterasu-o-mi-kami, commissioned her grandson, Ninigi, to descend to earth, carrying the sacred imperial symbols of jewel, mirror, and sword, to bring peace and tranquility to the divine land then torn with strife and dissension. As a distinctly modern touch, it may be noted in passing that Ninigi, when not actively engaged in pacifying the land, appears to have spent no inconsiderable part of his leisure corrupting the morals of practically every comely maiden who crossed his path.

* * *

. . . The historical background for the significant revival, during the Tokugawa period, of interest in ancient

Shinto doctrine was provided by scholars working under the direction of Mitsukuni, the Daimyo of Mito (1622–1700). To the library which he had inherited from his grandfather, Tokugawa Iyeyasu, Mitsukuni added old books acquired from many sources. Thereafter, with the aid of numerous scholars, he began the writing of the *Dai Nihon-shi,* or History of Great Japan. This monumental history, which is still of major importance, stressed the origin of the imperial line, emphasized the principles of legitimate succession, and placed the emperor in the forefront of national development. From the work of the Shinto historians many nationalists subsequently derived their fanatical reverence for the Throne.

Parallel with and in some degree influenced by the antiquarian studies of the Mito school of historians was the work of a line of scholars known as Wagakusha [scholars of Japanese learning] who, beginning in the seventeenth century, raised the standard of revolt against Chinese influence in Japanese life and thought. These scholars turned their attention to such long-forgotten works as the *Kojiki,* the *Nihonshoki,* and the *Manyoshu* [Collection of Myriad Leaves], the latter being an anthology of Japanese poetry belonging chiefly to the Nara period. Two lines of thought, both important for our purposes, were accepted by practically all of the scholars of the Wagakusha school. In the first place, they emphasized the Heavenly commission of a line of emperors, divine in origin, to rule over the land created by the gods and under the favored protection of the gods. Motoori Norinaga (1730–1801) declared that Japan was the land which had given birth to Amaterasu, the Sun Goddess, which "fact" proved its superiority over all other countries. The Sun Goddess, having endowed her grandson, Ninigi no Mikoto, with the three sacred treasures, proclaimed him and his descendants sovereigns of Japan for ever and ever.

From the central truth that Japan was the land of the gods, and its rulers the direct descendants of the gods, was derived the second tenet upon which the Shinto scholars unanimously agreed. Politically and culturally, Japan, the divine land, was immeasurably superior to her neighbors, and all foreign countries were bound to render homage to the Japanese sovereign and pay tribute to him. [Kamo] Mabuchi (1697–1769) pointed out that the benighted Chinese for ages past, unlike their Japanese neighbors, had had a succession of different dynasties to rule over them, each new dynasty being founded on rebellion and parricide. Seeking to discredit adherents of the Confucian school in Japan, Mabuchi declared that a philosophy which produced such results must be a false system. . . .

Another of the Wagakusha scholars, Hirata Atsutane (1776–1843), argued that Japan lay at the summit of the globe, all other countries having been formed at a much later period. Foreign countries were of course produced by the power of the creator gods, but they were not begotten by the original creators, Izanagi and Izanami, nor did they give birth to the Sun Goddess; hence their inferiority. The fact is patent, therefore, that the Mikado is the true Son of Heaven, who is entitled to reign over the four seas and the ten thousand countries. Hirata insisted, further, not merely that Japan was the land of the gods, but that her inhabitants were all descendants of the gods. Between the Japanese people and the Chinese, Hindus, Russians, Dutch, Siamese, Cambodians, and other peoples of the world there was a difference of kind rather than degree. It was not out of vain-glory alone that the Japanese called their country the land of the gods. For the gods who created all countries, belonging without exception to the Divine Age, were all born in Japan. Thus Japan was their native country, all the world acknowledging the appropriateness of the title.

The best of these Wagakusha scholars sought merely freedom from the dead weight of Chinese philosophy which was considered to be a burden upon the Japanese mind. The worst of them were, on the other hand, bigoted reactionaries and narrow-minded patriots who derided all things Chinese in order to enhance the glory of all things Japanese. In their patriotic zeal to discredit the culture of China, some of these writers descended to levels which can scarcely be called creditable. Mabuchi insisted that the Chinese were bad at heart, in spite of the teaching which they got, their bad acts being of such magnitude that society was thrown into disorder. Motoori referred repeatedly to the "vicious nature of the Chinese" which necessitated ethical teachings of which the spontaneously good Japanese had no need. Lao Tzu, he declared, was born "in a dirty country not under the special protection of the Sun Goddess." According to Hirata, the immeasurable superiority of the Japanese people to the natives of other countries in courage and intelligence stemmed from their divine descent.

Aside from the Mito school of historians and the Wagakusha scholars, other influences operated during the middle of the nineteenth century to impress upon the Japanese the sacred character of their empire and its divine ruler and, as a corollary, Japan's Heaven-bestowed destiny in the world. One of the most potent of these influences, having regard to ultimate consequences, was the teaching of Yoshida Shoin, a youthful samurai of the Choshu clan, who was executed in 1859, when he was but twenty-nine years old, for complicity in a plot to murder one of the shogun's officials in Kyoto.

Foreshadowing the Imperial Restoration of January 1868, Yoshida Shoin taught reverence for and undivided loyalty to the Emperor and respect, amounting almost to religious worship, for the Land of the Gods over which the Emperor reigned. In this respect his convictions approximated those of the Mito historians, although Shoin was not himself an adherent of that school. For our purpose, what is important in his conception of Japan's place in a system of international relationships. He was aware that the English were then invading the East. India had already fallen

under their control, China would be the next to be humiliated, and thereafter the "poison" of English influence and strength would spread to the Liuchiu Islands and Nagasaki. Self-defense, however, was not enough. From his reading of Japanese history, Shoin recalled the emperors of ancient times, "how their power was feared by foreigners, how their favor extended to other peoples, and that their great plans and strategy shine throughout a thousand generations. . . ." He therefore advocated the acquisition of Kamchatka and the Kurile Islands. The Koreans must be compelled to pay tribute to Japan "as in former times";[1] in addition, Formosa, the Liuchiu Islands, and part of Manchuria were deemed suitable for the extension of the Heavenly task. This territorial expansion, Shoin professed to believe, would serve the double purpose of holding Russia and America at a distance and humiliating them, and of compensating at the same time for the damage which their commerce would do to Japan. As a concrete first step, he advocated the seizure of an island off the coast of Korea as a measure preparatory to military operations on the continent. On another occasion he advocated the annexation of the islands to the south and their use as a base for an attack upon India.

The effect which Yoshida Shoin's teaching had upon the Choshu samurai can scarcely be overestimated. Among the students who sat at his feet, sipping the heady wine of imperial destiny,

[1] According to Dr. Kuno, all standard Japanese histories agree that for a period of at least 200 years, ending 663–668, Japan held suzerain power in one or another of the Korean states then existing. However, Japanese, Chinese, and Korean historians are agreed that after the destruction of the Kingdom of Kudara in 663, and the Kingdom of Korai in 668, the Japanese were compelled to abandon completely their suzerain claims in the peninsula. "None of the Chinese, Japanese, or Korean histories states that during the period of approximately thirteen hundred years beginning in the latter part of the seventh century Japan ever claimed suzerainty over Korea; nor do they state that Korea ever sent tribute to Japan." Yoshi S. Kuno, *Japanese Expansion on the Asiatic Continent* (Berkeley, 1937), I, 234. . . .

were men who were later to become powerful and famous. Yamagata Aritomo, who organized Japan's modern army and died both a prince and a Genro, was one of them. Two others were Ito Hirobumi, who likewise gained princely honors and the status of Genro, and Kido Koin [Takayoshi], whose untimely death in 1877 cut short a career that promised to be as significant as Ito's was to be. After Shoin's execution, Ito and Kido took his body and buried it.

One can see in the disputes over foreign policy after 1871 some of the effects which Shoin's teaching, and others like it, had upon the minds of the western clansmen who were then in control of the Japanese government. Some, making capital of the snubs administered by Korean officials to Japanese missions which had been sent to the peninsula, strongly favored an attack upon Korea, even if such action meant conflict with China. At the same time, Japanese claims to the Liuchiu Islands were asserted vigorously while similar and equally valid Chinese claims were denied. By 1879 the latter policy culminated, despite Chinese objections, in the formal incorporation of the Liuchius into the Japanese Empire. The Korean problem, however, required somewhat more cautious handling. Fearing the complications which might result, the opponents of a strong policy toward Korea persuaded their colleagues in the government to delay the ultimate decision until the return of the Iwakura mission, then in Europe. Lord Iwakura and his associates returned to Japan in September, 1873. Of the members of the mission, Ito had already, during a previous visit to England, seen and heard enough to appreciate both the strength and the ambitions of the Western powers. From their more recent survey of conditions in the United States and Europe, the other members of the mission, including particularly Kido Koin of Choshu and Okubo Toshimichi of Satsuma, had reached the conclusion that it would be well for Japan to tread softly. A war with Korea, which might involve China, would bankrupt the government and

leave the empire, financially and otherwise, so weak that it might easily fall a prey to the land-hungry nations of Europe. These and other arguments were heard in the debates which took place in the Council of State between October 14 and 23, 1873. The debate resulted in a victory for the advocates of internal reform, the consequence being that the opposing faction withdrew from the government.

As a sop to the expansionists, sanction was given in the spring of 1874 to an expedition to Formosa, where savage headhunters, in December, 1871, had massacred a considerable number of shipwrecked Liuchiuan sailors over whom the Japanese government claimed jurisdiction. When the Chinese government somewhat belatedly asserted exclusive jurisdiction over Formosa and began to make military preparations, Okubo was sent to Peking to liquidate the Formosan expedition on whatever terms were possible. A satisfactory settlement was reached October 31, 1874, and by December the Japanese troops were out of the island. Thus expediency dictated a postponement until 1894 of the fulfillment of Yoshida Shoin's dreams of empire. The reorganized Japanese government, set up in 1874, was dominated by men who had traveled with Lord Iwakura. They realized that before attempting to challenge the West, Japan would need a modern army and navy, railroads, factories, schools, and modern banking and currency system. With that work the Japanese leaders occupied themselves during the next two decades.

The work of the Mito school of historains, the Shinto theologians, and Yoshida Shoin had produced what might be called the messianic complex of the Japanese—their sense of divine destiny and their conviction that they were infinitely superior to their less-favored neighbors. . . . The discovery that Japan was considered not even an equal, much less a superior, in the family of nations, motivated the amazing transformation to which the empire was subjected after 1873, together with the determined movement for treaty revision which culminated in the British commercial treaty of 1894. The same determination to achieve equality among the nations was responsible very largely for the Sino-Japanese War of 1894–95. . . .

In order to gain this equality of status, achievements in the arts of peace were not enough. Railroads, a telegraph and postal system, schools, hospitals, factories, modern law courts, and even a Western parliament indicated the adaptability of the Japanese to the ways of the modern world. In spite of these achievements, and in part perhaps because of them, the Western world continued to look upon Japan as an interesting and clever child, precocious, but never for a moment to be taken seriously. Knowledge of this attitude of patronage and condescension was not concealed from the Japanese. They were aware, indeed, that in the West power was the test of national greatness. Very well, then, they would give a demonstration of their power. That China was the unwilling and incompetent sparring partner in this conflict was merely incidental. What was important was the fact that, by victory in a war, whether against China or any other nation, the Japanese demonstrated that, by the tests of power politics which prevailed in the West, they were entitled to that position of equality which they coveted.

Hyman Kublin

RESPONSE TO WESTERN AGGRESSION

Hyman Kublin (1916–   ), professor of Japanese history at Brooklyn College, the City University of New York, has written extensively on Meiji foreign policy, military reforms, and the early socialist movement. The following article was published fourteen years after World War II, in which Professor Kublin served as a lieutenant (j.g.) in the United States Navy. It differs sharply from Pollard's in its selection of evidence and in its analysis of Japan's traditional history. Kublin argues that Japan, conditioned by isolation and seclusion in the Tokugawa era, had no recent and scarcely even a remote colonial past to prepare it for a modern career in empire. On the contrary, it was a latecomer to such ventures. Whatever expansionist memories or sentiments survived from earlier times were the vague dreams of a few individuals and not the policy of the Tokugawa government. Japan's actions in the subsequent Meiji period must therefore be viewed as the result of a practical, empirical response to new problems, the most pressing being Western expansion in Asia. Kublin further argues that Japanese colonialism had its true origins in the aftermath of the Sino-Japanese war with the acquisition of Formosa in 1895. Earlier activities in Hokkaido, the Ryukyus, and the Bonin Islands were not full-blown imperialist ventures but modest expansion aimed at the reclamation and development for security reasons of frontier lands to which Japan had legitimate historical claims. Before 1895, the best means of defense seemed to lie in limited expansion coupled with a strong military establishment. After 1895, it appeared to depend upon entry into the ranks of the world powers.

REFLECTING upon the career in the colonial government of Formosa that was to win him world-wide fame in the early twentieth century, Baron Goto Shimpei[1] once remarked that "Japan had made no preparations whatever for the administration of the island at the time of its acquisition." Underscoring this neglect, he added, was "the fact that, in the case of other nations confronted by a similar occasion, elaborate schemes are generally formulated to meet contingencies connected with the occupation of a new territory." One may wonder whether the Baron included among the "elaborate schemers" the "absent-minded" builders of the British Empire.

It does not matter whether Baron Goto was aware of the complex historical processes, of the actions and accidents, involved in the creation of great empires. It is not even important whether he really believed that the colonial programs of the imperial powers were, like the war plans carefully devised by army general staffs, drawn from secret files as occasions demanded. Goto was primarily interested in the formulation and implementation of a colonial policy for Japan. His observation on his government's lack of preparedness to assume control and direction of Formosan affairs should thus be taken not simply as a confession and condemnation but rather as a statement of purpose.

[1] Gotō was head of the Civil Administration Bureau in Taiwan under Governor General Kodama Gentarō, 1898–1906. Subsequent positions included the presidency of the South Manchurian Railway and governorship of Tokyo. [Editor's note.]

From Hyman Kublin, "The Evolution of Japanese Colonialism," *Comparative Studies in Society and History*, II (1959), 67–70, 72–76, 79–82.

The real problem confronting Baron Goto was that Japan was a latecomer to the contest for overseas empire. Unlike the nations of western Europe, whose far-flung imperial dominions had been acquired over great or less periods of time since the sixteenth century, Japan's imperial holdings at the dawn of the twentieth century consisted of little more than a semi-savage island acquired but a few years before as a fruit of war. Whatever experience Japan had known in overseas expansion and settlement lay, moreover, in so remote a past as to be more an historical memory than a colonial tradition. Furthermore, the Japanese possessed neither a literature on colonial affairs, a policy to guide their efforts in their new overseas territory, nor a class of administrators trained in the government and exploitation of other men. On the surface, Japan's venture into the business of colonialism at the turn of the present century appeared extremely unpromising.

Yet, the builders of modern Japan's colonial structure worked with many advantages. They did not, on the one hand, have to contend with the inertia, dead-weight, and accumulated debris of imperial systems that had literally grown like Topsy nor was it necessary for them to cope with the manifold vested interests created in an extended process of historical change. They did not inherit the abuses and mistakes entrenched by time in almost every colonial administration nor did they possess the biases and illusions of peoples old and complacent in the ways of empire. Japan's pioneer colonial policy-makers were, on the other hand, able to avail themselves of the best experience accumulated by the imperial powers over the course of several centuries and by discriminate selection to secure the knowledge and technique promising the success of their efforts.

. . . Easy, if at times misleading, as it may be to generalize about the colonial systems which rest upon empires created throughout the world during the age of expansion, it is apparent that basic inspirations and motives for their creation have historically varied. What is of particular significance, however, is that few of the drives which culminated in colonialism in America, Africa, and Asia before the nineteenth century may be detected in the more recent Japanese activity. European expansion to and colonization of other lands was for long generated by scientific intellectual curiosity, by the frustrations and daring of merchant adventurers, and by the naked greed of established élite classes. The conquest and settlement of areas remote from mother countries were, in addition, sparked by religious dissidence in Europe, by evangelical and missionary fervor, and by the quest of emigrants for the political and economic opportunities closed to them at home. As a consequence of these various impulses, traditions and practices of international and intercontinental mobility were well established among Europeans by the late nineteenth century and colonialism was accepted by many peoples as a normal aspect of national affairs.

In Japan colonialism was to follow a course of development significantly different from the western European patterns. Though Japan was a late arrival on the scene of imperialism, it was for reasons dissimilar to German and Italian, not to speak of American, experiences. The inescapable fact is that Japanese history from the middle of the seventeenth to the middle of the nineteenth century had in several fundamental respects no counterpart in Europe. Not only did the Japanese confront for long a Chinese Empire dominating Eastern Asia and its outlying areas but their own abortive efforts had convincingly demonstrated the folly of expansionist ventures. But of infinitely greater importance was the policy of national isolation and seclusion deliberately pursued, and with astonishing consistency, by the government of Japan from 1640 to 1854.

. . . During Tokugawa times national seclusion was gradually to become more than a demand of the law; it was to develop into a tradition with a sanctity and an orthodoxy of its own. Given the existing system of political control and military power, this tradition could, in the final analysis, be challenged and changed only by those who upheld it. Nevertheless, the policy inherited by successive generations of Tokugawa shoguns was so strongly rooted that its ultimate modification and abandonment were to necessitate the invoking of a primary purpose of the policy, namely, the security and welfare of the country.

*   *   *

. . . The years between the abandonment of Tokugawa isolation and the final commitment to colonialism, embracing roughly the last half of the nineteenth century, were a critical era of transition for Japan. It was during this period, as in Germany, Italy, and to some extent the United States, that a multitude of relatively autonomous states were to be forged into a more centralized political organism, that the fires of nationalism were to be vigorously stoked, and that expansion towards newly claimed political frontiers was to occur. These were years when new dimensions were to be given to the political concept of Japan, when visions of an even greater Japanese Empire were to be stirred, and when the basis of a Japanese "irredentism" was to be laid. The years from Commodore Perry to the Treaty of Shimonoseki were, accordingly, if not consciously preparatory, nevertheless formative for Japanese colonialism.

The era of transition to colonialism was initiated with the severe shock to Tokugawa foreign policy delivered by Commodore Perry's naval-diplomatic mission in 1853. The ensuing struggle for decision within Japan understandably soon resolved itself into a problem of national security. Other motives of the contending factions apart, it is clear that concern for the defense of the land pervaded the various and conflicting proposals submitted by the Shogunate and the many feudal lords. Of all the centers of feudal power, however, the Shogunate was the most realistic in recognizing that the abandonment of the isolationist policy was both necessary and inevitable and that a radically new point of departure in matters of foreign policy had to be established. The Tokugawa were, however, to discover too late that their decision meant the destruction of the political and social system essential to their own survival.

It is an irony of history, if a commonplace of power politics, that the foreign policy of the Shogunate, which had aroused such bitter opposition amongst the feudal clans of the southwest, was to be adopted in its essentials once Tokugawa rule had been destroyed. In the same way that Shogunal policy after the conclusion of the Perry Treaty emanated from apprehension over western aggression, so too the foreign policy of the new government of the Meiji Emperor, established in 1868, was to a large extent founded on fear. The vigor of its activities notwithstanding, the Meiji regime was for long to be on the defensive in its international relations, its practical objectives being the maintenance of peace, the observation but ultimate abolition of the so-called "unequal treaties," and a modest expansion aimed at the promotion of the national security.

Only when the vital but limited goals of its foreign policy are borne in mind is it possible to understand the expansionist activities of the early Meiji government. In moving into and establishing or strengthening its authority in the Bonin islands, Okinawa, Hokkaido, and the Kuriles during the first decade of the Restoration era the central government of Japan had no thought of embarking upon a career in empire and colonialism. Possessing or inheriting claims of varying validity to sovereignty over these islands, the Meiji leaders viewed their actions as a reassertion and clarification of authority rather than as the annexation and conquest of alien lands and peoples. Despite the misleading terminology of the times, neither the Bonins, Okinawa, nor Hokkaido was considered by government officials to be a colonial area nor its settlers and inhabitants to be colonial subjects.[2] As a consequence, these outlying islands were to be administered in ways completely different from territories later annexed into the Japanese Empire.

Allowing for technical differences in constitutional and legal status, Japanese policy towards Okinawa and the Bonins was for many years to be suggestive of the treatment accorded Hawaii, Guam and Puerto Rico by the United States. But while American attitudes and behavior towards their insular possessions were primarily the product of indifference, Japanese policy in their southern islands was largely dictated by the poverty of the mother country. It was a rare Meiji oligarch who would have disputed the need for vigorous development programs in the Bonins, Okinawa, and Hokkaido but, considering the tremendous modernization enterprises under way in the homeland, it was evident that the required financial and economic resources were not available. Before very long, however, the course of international developments helped to resolve the dilemma and to establish the scale of priorities in Japan's program of overseas development efforts.

When the early Meiji government proclaimed its sovereignty over the Bonins and Okinawa, it had cause to believe that its claims would not be unchallenged. As it became increasingly evident that Japanese sovereignty over the Bonins would not be contested by the United States and Great Britain and that Chinese claims to Okinawa would not be aggressively pressed, Japan's minimum objectives of security in these areas were thereby fulfilled. Resting content with acknowledged possession of these islands, the Meiji government was able to pursue a "holding action" in the south, the development of the Bonin Islands and Okinawa being postponed to a more propitious time. Until the Sino-

Japanese War of 1894–95 the Bonin Islands were, consequently, as little known to most Japanese as are the Virgin Islands to present-day Americans, while in Okinawa this period of Japanese rule was to be dubbed the "Do-Nothing Era."

As opposed to its somewhat lackadaisical policy towards the Bonins and Okinawa, the Restoration government was alert, even before the Shogunate had been completely destroyed, to the need for positive action in Hokkaido. Here, at the "Northern Gate to the Empire," it was well understood that a bastion against Russian expansion in the northern Pacific would have to be constructed. The activities of other western powers in China, Southeast Asia, and India may well have caused chronic uneasiness among the Meiji leaders but the confrontation of Russians and Japanese in the northern islands, it was quickly realized, posed an immediate and critical problem. No elaborate explanation was thus required when the colonization and defense of Hokkaido were given top priority in the government's development programs.

Had any nation of the late nineteenth century but Japan undertaken a venture of the proportions of the Hokkaido colonization project, scarcely a ripple of international interest would probably have been aroused. That Japan, whose own economic modernization had not as yet advanced beyond the stage of mere ambition, could seriously plan to uplift as culturally and economically "primitive" an area as Hokkaido is ample testimony to her desperate concern for security. . . .

. . . Japanese colonialism, as we have known it in our times, had its origins in the aftermath of the Sino-Japanese War. It is not necessary to determine here whether Japan conspired to ·seize the great island of Formosa from China in 1894–95; it is most likely she did not. What is germane is that, when Japan acquired sovereignty over the tropical island by the Treaty of Shimonoseki, she encountered the problems which were to become typical in their colonial endeavors in the twentieth century. It

[2] The Japanese expressions *kaitaku* and *shokumin* may both be translated as "colonization." The former term has, however, the connotation of "reclamation" or "development," while the latter implies settlement of an alien territory. In speaking of their activities in the Bonins, Okinawa, and Hokkaido the Japanese customarily used the term *kaitaku*.

was, moreover, in Formosa that Japan was to create the pattern of colonialism which was, with the addition of subsequent more sophisticated glosses, to be applied in the administration and exploitation of such later conquests as Korea and Manchuria.

Whatever her reasons for acquiring Formosa may have been, events were rapidly to demonstrate that Japan did not know for some time what to do with her new possession. Entailed was a crucial problem somewhat similar to that which the United States was to face a few years later when the Philippines were annexed. The Japanese government had, in short, to determine whether it wished to become engaged in the prospectively profitable but potentially troublesome business of colonialism. At the time Formosa was considered to be as great a military and strategic liability as an asset, while, apart from a noisome carpet-bagging element in Japan, responsible political and business leaders were chary of a commitment to an area notorious for its political instability and economic stagnancy. Until the Japanese government reached a final decision on the disposition of Formosa, there could, thus, prevail no colonial policy worthy of the name and Japanese efforts, largely of an *ad hoc* nature, were to be devoted to the pacification of the island by a military regime.

In view of the purpose which Formosa was later to serve in the Japanese Empire, it is easy to overlook what may well have been a compelling reason for Japan's decision to embark upon a career in colonialism and, moreover, literally to dedicate herself to the achievement of success according to the prevailing standards of imperialism. Desirous of securing unqualified acceptance as a great power, of becoming the "Great Britain of the East," Japanese leaders may well have feared that, if they failed to respond to the challenges which empire posed, admission to the ranks of the world's élite might be delayed. A mere glance at the foreign press was enough to reveal the firm doubts entertained about Japan's, or any Asian nation's capacity to become

a successful colonizing power. National pride, whetted by the sneers and disparagement of western commentators upon the Far Eastern scene, may well have been crucial in shaping Japan's final decision on colonialism.

*   *   *

. . . Japan's last great venture in colonialism before 1931, when the initiative in expansionism was to be seized and held by aggressive militarists, was the annexation of Korea in 1910. As opposed to Formosa, possession of which had been acquired without much forethought, the extension of Japanese control over Korea represented the final solution to a problem which had been discussed and debated since the early years of the Meiji era. The nature of Japanese interest in the peninsula country, at first strategic and then increasingly economic, had rarely aroused broad differences of opinion among the leaders of the Meiji government; Korea had rather raised the question of the method of fulfillment of these interests. Successive victories in war with China and Russia removed all lingering doubts.

Having been deeply involved in Korean affairs for more than a generation before their annexation of the country the Japanese knew Korea as they had not known Formosa. In Korea there was to be little vacillation and indecision, no searching and groping for techniques of administration and exploitation, for the colonial policy and practice that had been forged in the crucible of Formosa were found to be generally adequate. Thus, though the Japanese were for a brief while to toy with a protectorate, their inability completely to control the country by indirect rule, the persistence of local opposition, and the logic of their own colonial convictions were to lead to the utter destruction of the Korean monarchy. If, as a result, Japanese rule in Korea until the end of World War II was to differ from that in Formosa, it was not in essence but rather in scale.

Korea was never permitted by the Japanese to exist as a mere excrescence of empire. Like Formosa, the old "Hermit

Kingdom" was also expected to submerge its identity in and to have no interests apart from those of its imperial sovereign. And when Koreans, renowned for their stubbornness, refused to play the role cast for them by their conquerors, they were ruthlessly and brutally hammered into submission and compressed into a system of political and police control far more effective, because of its technological superiority, than anything the Japanese themselves had known in Tokugawa times. During an age, moreover, when many of the colonial administrations throughout the world were being modified in response to the pressures of their subject peoples, Japan increasingly foisted upon her newest colony an apparatus of soldiers, policemen, bureaucrats, technicians, and teachers to guide the Koreans in the proper fulfillment of their duties as obedient and productive subjects of the Emperor. For sheer effectiveness of political control no other colony of the twentieth century ever approximated Korea, a prototype in many ways of the police states which were to emerge in the aftermath of World War I. . . .

The absorption of Korea represented the culmination of a distinct phase in the evolution of Japanese colonialism. Under the leadership of oligarchic bureaucrats powerfully influenced by their own peculiar historical traditions, by their hopes and ambitions for personal and national advancement, and especially by their fears for their country's future, an empire of modest territorial proportions was created in the peripheral areas of the Japanese archipelago. This empire, pieced together from "no-man's islands" on the sea frontier to north and south and particularly from satellites of the decaying Chinese Empire, was far more compact than any other imperial regime of the twentieth century. Relatively easy to control with the military and police forces of the homeland, the Japanese Empire, which embodied the hopes and anxieties of Meiji Japan itself, excited the dread and antagonism only of its despoiled and chastened neighbors but scarcely the envy and concern of the richer and stronger imperial powers of the times. If there existed any grave danger to the perpetuation of this empire, it lay perhaps in a Japanese appetite for overseas territory increasingly whetted by Japanese imperial success.

Among the many empires of the late nineteenth and early twentieth centuries the Japanese was in many ways unique. What distinguished it primarily was neither its size nor location, neither the composition of its peoples nor the manner of its creation, which was decidedly conventional in an age of rampant imperialism. Of paramount significance was perhaps the Asian provenance of this empire. For, although imperial regimes had risen and fallen in the East for several millenia, the phenomenon of an expanding Asian empire in an era when the western powers were engaged in the obliteration of national independence in Asia was clearly extraordinary.

William G. Beasley

A QUESTION OF TIMING AND NOT OF GOALS

Professor Beasley (1919–   ) stands between the two extremes expressed in the preceding selections; there was an expansionist tradition, but it is often exaggerated or misunderstood. Along with many other scholars, he agrees that the crucial test of Japanese designs and latent ambitions came in 1873 when critics of the Meiji government, as well as many persons within it, demanded military intervention in Korea. The motives of all parties to the dispute were complicated, but in the end the advocates of caution won their case and control of the government. Until 1894, the emphasis was on restraint abroad and reform at home. The decision of 1873 is therefore viewed as central to a proper understanding of the rate and the nature of early Meiji modernization. This is not to argue that expansionism in itself was condemned in 1873 as inherently immoral or impractical, or that the Meiji statesmen were without imperialist ambitions. According to Beasley, whose assessment rests upon a broad view of the whole of nineteenth-century Japanese diplomacy, 1873 really meant caution now and conquest later. In the meantime, the government should allow small advances to satisfy ambition and above all to placate the opposition. Those out of power often used foreign policy to attack or embarrass the government. Those in power, although usually less emotional and chauvinistic, tended to sanction as much of the extremist policies as they could in order to undercut the critics and cling to power. The following comments are taken from Beasley's inaugural address, May, 1955, as Professor of the History of the Far East, School of Oriental and African Studies, University of London.

IT was only in 1853, with the arrival of Commodore Perry and his demand for the conclusion of a treaty between America and Japan, that the challenge [to Japan's seclusion] became immediate and practical. It was at this point, one might say, that modern Japanese foreign policy begins. On the other hand, the debates which had preceded it among those who were comparatively well informed are vital to an understanding of later Japanese diplomacy, for they established a pattern of ideas which was to become widespread by 1858 and continued to influence policy for half a century thereafter.

*   *   *

. . . Broadly speaking, in the middle years of the century controversy centered on two opposing slogans: that of *jōi*, or "expel the barbarians," and that of *kaikoku*, or "open the country." Ostensibly they are direct and unambiguous, apparently irreconcilable. In fact, each represents a wide variety of opinion, sometimes overlapping and always shifting with the progress of events, so that it is often difficult to draw a clear line of demarcation between the two. The label *kaikoku* is most frequently applied to the small group of men who saw Japan's hope for the future in an extensive policy of Westernization which would enable her at last to meet the West on equal terms; but it included also those, both numerically and politically more important to whom opening the ports was no more than a grudging recognition of superior force. Advocates of expulsion were just as varied in their

From W. G. Beasley, *The Basis of Japanese Foreign Policy in the Nineteenth Century* (University of London: School of Oriental and African Studies, 1955), pp. 6, 8–9, 11, 14–22, 26.

outlook. At one extreme stood the majority of the lesser samurai, restless and dissatisfied in an age of growing economic hardship, conditioned to a belief in the virtues of seclusion, and ready to blame the foreigners—once the ports were open—for most of the ills of Japanese society. These were the men whose readiness to use the sword, both on foreigners and on Japanese who had dealings with them, caused crisis after crisis in the ten years after 1858. At the other end of the scale were those whose *jōi* views, however violent the language in which they were expressed, retained at least a semblance of realism. Japan, they agreed, would have to adopt Western weapons and techniques to make defense successful; but if in the process she permitted trade on an important scale, still more if she permitted the adoption of Western religion and ideas, then her society would be corrupted and she would have destroyed the very thing which it was her object to preserve. To some, such reasoning would even justify a war to keep the Powers from gaining foothold in Japan. To others, especially to the leaders of the *jōi* movement, it involved no more than a stubbornness in negotiation greater than anything envisaged by those who recognized the need for opening ports.

If one reads the documents of the period, it soon becomes clear that some of the ideas which we call *jōi* and some which we call *kaikoku* were closer to each other than the terms themselves would lead us to expect. Opinion, in fact, was not consolidated in two distinct and separate segments. It can better be described as a kind of spectrum, in which the colors, though distinguishable, merged gradually into each other over the whole of their total range.

Such a conclusion is not strikingly novel. It does need emphasis, however, for in studying the distribution of these ideas within Japan it can only produce distortion if we seek to fit them to a framework imposed by inherited and largely artificial labels. We must recognize, for example, that the views a Japanese expressed were greatly influenced by his degree of knowledge of the outside world. They were also related, under a feudal and authoritarian government, to the political status of the individual, especially to the ease with which he could obtain information about defenses and finance. No man who recognized the essential weakness of Japan's position could long continue to advocate recourse to war. Certainly very few officials did so, whatever their distaste for foreign intercourse. When it came to formulating policy, the knowledge and responsibility which went with office were usually enough to tip the scales against the dictates of emotion.

*   *   *

. . . [I]f responsibility imposed moderation on some, lack of it enabled others to adopt a position more in keeping with their own beliefs and predilections. This holds good for extremists of either group, whether *jōi* or *kaikoku*. Men who desired the exclusion or expulsion of the foreigners were free to ignore the realities of international politics, or at least to assume that determination was an effective substitute for strength. Men who urged the government to enter into full and friendly relations with the West were able to overlook the difficulties which such a policy entailed at home. The two extremes, in fact, reflect the real nature of the Japanese government's dilemma. While foreign pressure pushed it in one direction, domestic opposition pushed it in another; and by the middle of the nineteenth century it was doubtful whether the Shogun still had the authority to impose an unpopular decision on the country.

*   *   *

The Meiji Restoration of 1868 opened a new chapter in Japanese history. Under the guise of restoring the Emperor's former privileges, much that was old was swept away and the ground was prepared for changes which were to prove revolutionary in their impact on society. The same process was eventually to make possible an entirely new approach to foreign policy. Yet for the first few years the course pursued by the Meiji government in its dealings with the Powers was remarkable not for its novelty but for its continuity with what had gone before. Despite the fact that the overthrow of the Tokugawa had all the appearance of a victory for the *jōi* party, Japan continued to observe her treaty obligations. She did so reluctantly, perhaps, but if anything with more assurance than in the past. Certainly she made no attempt to carry out expulsion, the policy with which the anti-Tokugawa party—now in power —had been so closely linked.

The reason for this is not far to seek. Japan had new leaders, it is true, men who were generally younger and more able than their predecessors. One would expect them to act with greater firmness and decision. This did not mean, however, that their actions would be such as to bring them into conflict with the West. Many of the group, and those the most influential, had long been convinced that any attempt to expel the foreigners was doomed to failure. It was a conviction which events had forced upon them; and after their assumption of office in 1868 it became impossible to conceal it. The public avowal of anti-foreign views, which had been so useful in their opposition to the Shogun, now became an embarrassment, if not a source of danger, for a dispute with the Powers might threaten both the country's safety and the government's stability. Before the Restoration they had been free to shape their statements on foreign policy exclusively with reference to politics within Japan. After it, they became subject to pressures arising from the international situation. As a result, the realism which already marked their private views had also to be reflected in their public actions.

The apparent volte-face which this entailed did not escape the notice of contemporaries. It contributed to the sense of frustration which was rapidly developing among those to whom expulsion was an article of faith, and thus played a part in diverting anti-foreign sentiment to other channels. For it was not only in the ideas of the leaders that

events were causing change. The bombardments of Kagoshima and Shimonoseki, the use of powerful squadrons to back the negotiations of 1865 and 1867, the continuing presence of British troops in Yokohama, all these brought home to a much wider public the catastrophic results that would follow from a use of force. On the other hand, recognition of this did not have the same effect on the many as on those who were in power. The dynamic content of the *jōi* movement had always been more emotional than rational; and the knowledge that expulsion was impossible did nothing to destroy the feelings which had made the movement strong. Indeed, it heightened them by emphasizing Japan's subservience to the West. So disillusion, far from pacifying discontent, served only to give it a new form: it expressed itself as a demand for expansion on the Asiatic mainland.

Such a demand, of course, was nothing new in Japanese history. From earliest times the Korean peninsula had been a scene for Japanese ambitions, intermittent though these were. Occasionally, when under the domination of more powerful neighbors, it had also seemed to be a threat to the safety of Japan. It was in this form that it had presented itself during the first half of the nineteenth century, with the difference that the danger came from Russia, not from China, and that Japan no longer possessed the means of defending herself against it. . . .

Even in this period, however, when there was a general preoccupation with the problem of defense, there were signs of something more positive in Japanese reactions. As early as 1825 it had been argued that Japan might find it necessary to intervene in China to organize resistance to the Western Powers. Less precise, but on the whole more widespread in Japan, was a vague desire for international recognition and prestige, evidence that there were some who looked beyond immediate dangers to a time when their country could do more than simply hold its own against encroachment. . . .

. . . Conquest, whether in Korea or

elsewhere, could serve a double purpose: first, by providing satisfaction for the country's injured morale; second, by giving Japan material advantages in her struggle against domination by the Powers. . . .

The importance and continuity of this tradition can easily be overemphasized. None the less, while it was not inevitable, at least it was not surprising that the frustration of *jōi* plans should have led discontent to seek its outlet in the idea of territorial expansion. Emotion, moreover, was reinforced by practical considerations. One of the strongest forces behind the anti-Tokugawa movement had been unrest among the lesser samurai, but very few of them had gained by its success. Many, indeed, were worse off than before. The reforms of 1868–71 robbed them of a privileged status in society and gave them nothing in return; and to men who suffered from this process overseas adventure had the merit of providing a solution to problems which were immediate and personal. The campaigns themselves would give employment to a military class which had no other function in society, while victory would bring land to serve as their reward.

By 1873, expansionist sentiment and samurai unrest had come together in a rising demand that Japan should take action against Korea; and they had influential spokesmen in the ruling group. The support of Saigō Takamori, in particular, far more than that of men like Itagaki, Etō, or Gotō, gave the movement a real political importance. For Saigō was the most popular of the Meiji leaders. In many ways, too, he was typical of samurai emotions and ideals. As a man of Satsuma he had played a major part in overthrowing the Tokugawa, but it had been his hope that this would make possible a regeneration of the feudal system, not its abolition, and he found himself increasingly out of sympathy with the modernizing tendencies of the new era. His Korean policy was a logical result. On the one hand, he saw it as a means of resolving personal conflicts, as the opportunity to die a soldier's death. On the other, he looked to a

Korean war as an instrument to retrieve the fortunes of his class. It would not only provide the samurai with employment and rewards, but also, by restoring them to their rightful place as the country's military leaders, it might give them once more a social and political status commensurate with their traditions. To Saigō, in fact, war was a way of reversing policy at home.

Inevitably, this brought opposition from other members of the government. Several of Saigō's colleagues had already begun to draft a program for the development of Japan which ran directly counter to the ideas he supported. Indeed, it found precedent only in the plans put forward by extreme *kaikoku* thinkers in the previous decade. What is more, largely as a result of the Iwakura mission of 1871–73, it was taking final shape at the time when the cry for expansion reached its loudest.

The Iwakura mission was in intention diplomatic, an embassy to the capitals of Europe and America which was designed as the first step towards revision of the treaties.[1] For this reason it included senior members of the new government: the court noble, Iwakura Tomomi at its head; and two of the most able of the samurai, Ōkubo Toshimichi and Kido Kōin. These men soon found that there was little hope of achieving the immediate object of their mission. More important, however, was the fact that in the eighteen months they spent outside Japan they saw at first hand— and for the first time—the full extent of the West's material progress. They came to realize that the purchase of a few warships and modern cannon would not of itself be enough to give Japan a measure of equality. So they returned home acutely aware of the ground that was still to be covered. Kido and Ōkubo, especially, had been convinced that only far-reaching reforms in Japan's political, economic, and military organization

[1] The embassy was in fact from the beginning both a diplomatic and a learning mission; its members wished to assess the prospects for treaty revision within a few years and above all to see and judge the Western world for themselves. [Editor's note.]

would make it possible to ensure her independence.

The policies which sprang from this decision came to the test in the autumn of 1873. During the mission's absence Saigō had dominated the inner councils of the government. He had therefore been able to secure a formal resolution in favor of an attack upon Korea, which was to be begun as soon as it had been approved by the envoys then in Europe. The news brought them quickly home; Ōkubo first, then Kido, and finally Iwakura. All of them were opposed to Saigō's plan, but it was left to Ōkubo, Saigō's rival for the loyalties of Satsuma, to take the lead in stating their objections. He did so in a long memorandum, written in October, which provides an interesting summary of the arguments for moderation. In the first place, it said, the country's finances would not stand the strain of foreign war. Any increase in expenditure would bring economic dislocation, which in turn would cause further disaffection and unrest, perhaps even to the point where it endangered the regime. Secondly, even were this contingency avoided, war would use up energy and resources which should properly be devoted to reform at home. It would mean postponement of the very measures on which Japan must ultimately depend to give her strength and status. Finally, war would increase the danger from the Powers. Once Japan was involved in a struggle with Korea, both Britain and Russia would be tempted to intervene and strengthen their position. This would end all hope of recovery for the future.

The debate which followed was long and acrimonious, but Ōkubo and Kido won the day. The decision to attack Korea was reversed, Saigō and his friends resigned from office, and the victors were left to work out their plans in greater detail. The result, at home, was the westernization of Japan. In foreign affairs, it was what one might call "the policy of restraint." In large measure this was to determine the actions of Japanese governments for twenty years thereafter.

The policy of restraint was a natural corollary of the domestic program of the Meiji leaders. It had as its primary object the achievement of treaty revision —to which part of domestic reform was also linked—and it was based on recognition of the fact that this could only be done by courtesy of the Western Powers, especially of Great Britain, whose influence had controlled the shaping of the treaties and without whose concurrence it was impossible to change them. In pursuit of this aim Japan must become not only strong but also "respectable": respectable as the West understood the term. She had to ensure observance of the treaties while they lasted, and enter as fully as possible into international agreements of a general kind. Above all, she had to avoid any action which ran seriously counter to the interests or susceptibilities of the Powers.

That this applied to direct relations with the West is obvious enough. Less obviously, it provides also the framework in which to set Japan's relations with her neighbors. For all that it was attractive, overseas adventure could be dangerous, both because it diverted energy from tasks at home and because it might involve the country in disputes for which it was unready. It followed that expansion of any major kind must be avoided, or at least postponed, until such factors ceased to operate. Even local gains were subject to the veto of the Powers. This was made clear in 1874, when there was a last-minute attempt to call off the expedition to Formosa because foreign envoys viewed the project with disfavor. On the other hand, where the West was approving or unconcerned there was every reason for seeking an advantage. Expansion was not in itself to be condemned. None of the arguments used in 1873 were aimed at the idea of Saigō's plan, only against its timing and appropriateness. Moreover, there were forces in domestic politics which gave the mainland an appeal even to those who felt the need for caution. Kido, for example, as early as 1869, had remarked that an attack on Korea would serve a useful purpose, for it would transfer the attention of the samurai from the domestic to the foreign scene, where they would no longer constitute a challenge to the government's authority. Ōkubo himself supported the expedition to Formosa, in the hope that it would reduce the resentment left by the Korean dispute some months earlier.

The policy of restraint, therefore, had two aspects. While it involved cooperation with the Powers and deference to their advice, it also aimed at making small advances which would help to satisfy ambition. . . .

. . . [H]owever, critics of the government's foreign policy, though defeated, were not silenced. On the contrary, support for the idea of expansion on the mainland continued to increase.

*   *   *

. . . Before the end of the century the gulf between the policies of government and those of opposition had begun to narrow. The appeal of expansion became greater as the opposition grew in power, while progress in reform at home and the increasing readiness of the Powers to grant Japan an equal status made restraint less necessary. With the Sino-Japanese War of 1894–95 Japan became an active participant in the affairs of northeast Asia. The change brought problems as well as obvious advantages. She was no longer a victim, but—in China, at least—a member of the club. As a result, her concern was less with defense than with the need to protect her interests overseas. This entailed a complete re-thinking of her relations with the Powers, especially with Russia and Great Britain, a process which was to lead at least to an Anglo-Japanese alliance and a Russo-Japanese war.

II. EXPANSION BY FORCE AND DIPLOMACY

John M. Maki

TRADITIONAL MILITARISM

To many scholars it seems obvious that Japan's military tradition predisposed it to war and conquest. For centuries, there had been a feudal and military society dominated by warriors. The values of all the classes had been heavily influenced by the warriors' code, bushidō. The people were conditioned to accept authoritarian rule. Japan had no need to learn the basic lessons of warfare from the Germans or the French but only modern techniques and refinements. The following comments by Professor Maki, taken from a book published shortly after the end of the Pacific War, are representative of this approach. He stresses that the Meiji changes of 1868 did not constitute a revolution. The new ruling group included many of the old warriors, but above all it perpetuated their ideas, methods of control, and psychology. It is nonsense to accept Japan's propaganda that the wars of 1894–95 and 1904–05 were wars of defense. They were waged to gain wealth and glory. War was the natural expression of an aggressive people organized in a military state. Professor Maki (1909–   ) taught for many years at the University of Washington and is now Vice-Dean of the College of Arts and Sciences at the University of Massachusetts. He is the author of several works on modern Japanese politics and foreign relations.

A RULING class, not a philosophy of government, came to an end with the collapse of the Tokugawa régime. The absolutism[1] of the old warrior oligarchy was retained as the basis of the new government. The Tokugawa *bakufu* was a government by warriors; the new state in Japan was an oligarchy dominated by militarists. The old class lines separating the warriors from the rest of Japanese society were broken down, but the warrior psychology was a powerful

motivation of the builders of the new Japan. The Meiji Restoration was organized primarily by men from the warrior class to further their own ends as members of a ruling oligarchy. As sweeping as the Restoration was, it left intact the basic political, economic, and social attitudes on which the old structure of government in Japan had rested.

The new Japan was not the child of revolution. The transition from the mediaeval to the quasi-modern was carefully controlled by the oligarchy. It retained control of the process of political change as it monopolized political power itself. Modern Japan arose out of the political strife of oligarchic faction against oligarchic faction, not out of a clash of class against class and ideology against ideology.

---

[1] Absolutism is a term employed with varying shades of meaning in modern Japanese history. Here it is a synonym for autocratic government, but in Marxist scholarship it generally has the technical meaning of control by an uneasy coalition of military and landed oligarchs who together prevent a full-scale social revolution from taking place. [Editor's note.]

From John M. Maki, *Japanese Militarism, Its Cause and Cure* (New York: Alfred Knopf, 1945), pp. 155–156, 182–185, 193–194.

The old feudal attitudes toward authority remained untouched. They were deliberately preserved in the face of all the changes that were being wrought in Japan, for they provided the perfect foundation for the obedience and subservience demanded of the subjects of new Japan. The old divisions between the classes were legally abolished, but the attitudes that were created by the class distinctions of the Tokugawa period continued.

Subservience to the state and obedience to its authority were sedulously cultivated by both education and indoctrination. State control of education guaranteed that the "proper" attitudes toward government would be cultivated among the young. Emperor worship and the glorification of the military ideal were constantly drummed into the ears of the people. The few who managed to gain a liberal education were stigmatized as being apostates who had deserted the true way of the Japanese subject. The great mass of the Japanese people was ready to accept Japanese totalitarianism both because it was a part of the Japanese tradition and because they were indoctrinated to accept it as the normal form of government.

The new machinery of government that was set up in Japan was authoritarian both in spirit and in form, although the dramatic contrast between it and the old Tokugawa absolutism tended to create the impression that it was both advanced and at least partially democratic. The Constitution, for example, was (and is)[2] a political instrument created by believers in authoritarian government and designed to keep control of Japan in the hands of the few, and to exclude popular participation.

*   *   *

. . . When the feudal period came to an end, the warriors lost their special privileges as a class, indeed they disappeared as a separate and distinct part of the population. But the ideology of

[2] A reference to the Meiji Constitution of 1889. [Editor's note.]

the class became that of the nation. Men whose ideas were essentially those of the vanished warrior class carried the largest share of the burden of building the new government in Japan. They constructed an authoritarian state that was ideally suited for purposes of war. What is perhaps even more important is the fact that they made Japan into a nation of warriors, not in the classical sense of the term as old Japan had understood it, but in the more dangerous sense, that all Japan accepted the ideals of war and its use as an instrument of national policy.

The whole concept of war and of the bearing of arms was changed with the fall of the Tokugawa shogunate and the collapse of the feudal order. No longer was the bearing of arms a jealously guarded privilege of a few select members of the population. Under the new system all men became soldiers. Mass conscription changed a mark of social distinction and political power into a duty and an obligation to the state.

The feudal order resulted naturally in the glorification of the warriors and all they stood for, but there were certain fundamental weaknesses in the system when viewed from the standpoint of men interested in the furtherance of war and militarism as instruments of national policy. The greatest fault of the warrior class, from this point of view, was the fact that it was not an army. In addition, the Tokugawa régime, although of, by, and for warriors, did not favour armies. Its control of the country was so complete that it did not require a large army in the formal sense of the term. It did not allow others to maintain armies, for they were dangerous to Tokugawa rule.

Even had it been possible to raise large bodies of men under the old régime, they still would have fallen far short of the demands of even nineteenth century warfare. They had no real weapons. The sword was still the weapon in which the warrior placed his greatest trust, although firearms had been imported in the sixteenth century. It was his "soul," and was regarded as his most prized possession. The Japanese had a few pieces of artillery, which had been built either on the model of the artillery pieces brought into the country in the late sixteenth century or had been cast under the direction of the Dutch who were allowed to remain in the country. These weapons were no match for what the West had developed. The bombardments of the Choshu forts and of Kagoshima in the 1860's were proof enough of that. Whatever faith in their traditional weapons might have lingered in the hearts of the warriors was certainly swept away in 1877, when an army of despised conscripts, armed with the best weapons in Japan, smashed the proud forces of the Satsuma clan which were still fighting more or less according to the old rules.

The system of universal male conscription, instituted in 1872, guaranteed that the army would be of the nation; for this meant that virtually no family would be without at least one member who was a trained soldier. Every able-bodied male knew that the state was going to demand that he devote time to learning the profession of the soldier. Women had to send their sons, fathers, brothers, and husbands off to fight and die for the country. Only by accident or ill fortune could one escape discharging this debt to the state.

Men were only one of the requirements of the new national army. It also needed modern arms, the factories that could make them, and a transportation system that could deliver them. The nation's economy was vitally affected by the development of the modern army. A large proportion of the civilian population contributed indirectly, as well as directly, to the maintenance of the army. Workers, contractors, businessmen, manufacturers, financiers, all had an interest one way or another in the Army and Navy. The nation had to pay for the new army, too. Much of the national budget was devoted to the building, arming, supplying, and maintenance of the Army and Navy.

Modern Japan had a national army, but this vast new organization because of its very extent had to be kept busy. An army not employed in the business of war would be a truly expensive luxury, so expensive that Japan, a relatively poor country, could not continue to support it. Popular discontent might even develop, if the people had to continue to pay heavy taxes in order to maintain an army that did not fight. Its very closeness to the mass of the people made it necessary for the rulers of Japan to find work for it to do.

In the early years of modern Japan the Army had perhaps its best justification. The stress and strain of the destruction of the feudal order and the shift to a quasi-modern state inevitably brought in its train dislocations which might have proved serious had not the government had under its control an army that was able to maintain relative peace and order within the country during those critical times. Japan also needed an army for protection from the threat outside her borders. For some time after the opening of the country there was danger that foreign arms might reduce Japan to the same semicolonial status that was rapidly being forced on China. These threats were enough to justify the building up of an extensive armed force.

By the 1880's foreign intervention in Japanese affairs had virtually disappeared, and the new structure was secure against any active internal opposition. But by that time the new armed strength of Japan was firmly established. All Japanese had a stake in it and all were involved one way or another in its operations. The passage of time and the grim succession of wars firmly fastened this new national army on the Japanese people and the Japanese state.

With the immediate need for a modern army eliminated, the Japanese government had to seek occupation for the Army. The leaders of the new Japan were not averse to such plans, for they were men who had been born and bred in an atmosphere of militarism. The Army was dominated by men from the Choshu clan, and the Navy by the Satsuma clan. With the armed forces of the country controlled by men from these warlike clans, it was to be expected that work would be found for them outside the country when their immediate utility at home had disappeared.

*   *   *

. . . [Japan's modern rulers further intensified] the spirit of militarism that had flowed through Japanese life as a strong and enduring current for many centuries. They made war acceptable to the Japanese people. But one of the greatest contributing factors to the rôle of war in modern Japan was the success that accrued to Japan as a result of the waging of war.

In the last half century Japan has averaged better than one major war a decade. The first Sino-Japanese War of 1894–5, the "Manchurian Incident" of 1931–2, and the current war which began in 1937, all involved China. The war of 1904–5 was against Russia. Japan's participation in the first World War was directed against Germany. Finally, late in 1941 Japan invaded Southeast Asia, the Philippines, the Netherlands East Indies, and the islands of the Southwest Pacific, a move which aligned all great powers save Russia and Germany against her.

These wars were not wars of defense, although they were treated as such in Japanese propaganda. They were wars of aggression, each of which added something to the wealth of Japan, temporarily at least. They were the logical expression in foreign affairs of the ideas of the authoritarian state. They were the extension beyond Japan's borders of the militarism that had so long been characteristic of Japan. Although there is no definite proof that the makers of modern Japan deliberately adopted war as an instrument of national policy, the manner in which each war led logically to the next hints strongly that there was a master-plan behind the whole program of conquest.

When one regards the great gains that Japan won by means of war, it is not surprising that the Japanese people developed a positive attitude toward it. It was through war that Japan gained international prestige, territory, raw materials, wealth, and glory. Until the war with China began in 1937 the Japanese people had every reason to believe that war was right, and that it was to their advantage to follow their military leaders into whatever venture they might attempt.

M. Frederick Nelson

THE CONFUCIAN WORLD ORDER

Japan learned quickly that the protection of its interests and the successful practice of international politics required a modern diplomatic establishment as well as a modern army and navy. The Ryukyu Islands, for example, were acquired by reliance upon international law and the display of force. In the closing years of the Meiji era, Japan concluded diplomatic alliances while stockpiling armaments. When Japan abandoned the Tokugawa policy of isolation, it also shed certain Confucian notions of world order on which the neighboring Chinese empire had been fashioned and which had been incorporated into its own version of Japanese Neo-Confucianism. Japan then set up a foreign office, organized a diplomatic and consular service, and mastered international law. By the turn of the century its diplomats were polished professionals. In his book on the old order in East Asia, the late M. Frederick Nelson (born 1907) has traced the evolution of the Chinese tribute system and its acceptance by the Koreans. He suggests that in theory and practice the Chinese order, although resting upon a superior-inferior pattern of relations, had as much ethical content to recommend it as had the Western state system, which assumes the equality of all states, rich or poor, large or small, and stresses the sanctity of national sovereignty. The clash of these notions in Korea contributed to the Sino-Japanese war. Korea, initially under duress but later by choice, had accepted a younger-brother relationship to China as its proper position in the natural order of things. Japan's insistence that Korea be independent of China was mischievous and harmful. Moreover, Japan misused international law in creating a new hegemony in East Asia based on repression and brutality, in effect distorting both the Eastern and Western orders. Nelson served with the Office of Strategic Services in World War II, and his book is based on doctoral research completed at Duke University one year before Pearl Harbor.

AS the Confucian culture became dominant in China and spread into the Korean peninsula, it conquered where armies had failed. In consequence of this phenomenon, the rulers of the petty Korean nations came to view investiture by the emperor of China, the Son of Heaven, as necessary to their right to rule, or as a delegation by the world ruler of the authority he possessed from Heaven. Viewing themselves as lesser members of the imperial family, these Korean rulers showed their respect by sending tribute to the Son of Heaven and accepting from him their investiture, along with gifts and admonitions concerning the preservation of the natural order.

When barbarians from the areas north and west of China succeeded in overthrowing the reigning Chinese dynasty, Korea, in accordance with the legitimism fundamental to Confucian teaching, gave up her allegiance to the orthodox Chinese rulers only under duress and returned to them at the first opportunity. The Mongols, for instance, being rejected as barbarians by the Koreans, found it most difficult to control the peninsula. Without the sanction of

From M. Frederick Nelson, *Korea and the Old Orders in Eastern Asia* (Baton Rouge: Louisiana State University Press, 1945), pp. 290–297.

the Confucian familial relationship, they had to use force and direct rule to hold Korea's allegiance.

After the last half of the fourteenth century the relations between Korea and China achieved a regularization which was disrupted only in the nineteenth century by contacts with the Western states. During this long period Korea was considered a lesser nation. The various lesser nations in the East Asiatic Confucian system[1] existed on a *fan-ch'en* basis, that is, as "border wardens" to the Middle Kingdom and its Son of Heaven, and they were termed *shu-pang* or dependent nations. Korea, as the closest of the *shu-pang*, stood in the relation to China as a younger to an elder brother, the latter also possessing, as head of the Confucian family of nations, the powers of the father. Consequently, the relations between these two nations were regulated, not by law, treaty, or agreement of any kind, but by *li*, the rules of proper conduct, which governed the five great relations that made up all social existence.

In this association China was to give the benevolent protection and advice that a parent or elder brother might properly give. Korea, in turn, owed that respect and submission which a younger brother or son should show to his elder brother or parents. There were, therefore, no definite legal limits concerning what China could or could not do. Legalistic formulation would merely have distorted the true relationship and prevented its adjustment to the varied situations of actual life. The relationship was natural, familial, not legal.

In times of peace, when no strain existed on the relationship, it was signalized by certain regular forms of intercourse such as the sending of tribute,

[1] At the beginning of the nineteenth century the lesser nations in the system were Korea, Liu-ch'iu, Annam, Laos, Siam, Burma, and Sula. Areas such as Tibet, Mongolia, and Turkestan were not separate nations but were governed more as provinces. Japan had at various times acknowledged and renounced an inferior status in the East Asiatic system. [In the nineteenth century, Japan was listed in Ch'ing dynasty annals as a trading nation, not a tribute country. (Editor's note.)]

the return of gifts, the dispatch of imperial missions to confer investiture or offer congratulations, and other acts of ceremony. When harmony existed these were the only outward tokens of the inward status of being a *shu-pang*, a nation related to China as a son or respectful younger brother to his father or elder brother. Just as ceremony alone marked the natural father's control over his son in ordinary circumstances, so China received only these outward tokens from Korea. Yet as the Chinese father in times of crisis had absolute control, even unto death, so the Chinese state in the nineteenth century exercised a like privilege in increasing her control over Korea. No legal contract was necessary for China to take such action; no legal contract fixed the limits to which she might go. Who could say, "This much aid shall the parent or elder brother give, and no more?"

When the Western states began their eastward march in the latter part of the nineteenth century, they brought with them a concept of "international law" which they considered to be universal in scope. In their attempts to deal with Korea, however, they found that a relationship existed between that country and China which they could not understand. Searching back into the categories which their international system listed, they hit upon that of suzerain and vassal as most nearly fitting this East Asiatic relationship, and they then proceeded to apply the legal attributes of vassalage to the non-legal status of a *shu-pang*. Since they understood that a suzerain always handles his vassal's foreign relations, when China refused responsibility for Korea's acts the Western states accepted the refusal as a renunciation of suzerainty. Therefore, particularly after China encouraged Korea to sign treaties with the West to balance power against power, Korea was viewed as sovereign and independent, and all Chinese claims concerning her were rejected as pure ceremony and of no legal effect.

China endeavored to have included in the early Western treaties a recognition of the Confucian relationship.

When this failed, she adopted the expedient of complementing each treaty with a letter attesting the inferior position of Korea with respect to that of the Middle Kingdom. But the admissions that the Korean king was *tzŭ chu* (master of himself) were translated into "independent" and "sovereign," and the Western states were thus further convinced of the lack of justification for China's claims. According to the non-legalist Confucian reasoning, however, Korea, the younger brother, was capable of being "master of himself" without renouncing his obligations to the elder brother, China.

With no competitors, China had been willing for centuries to exercise only the outward ceremonies of the central nation over its *shu-pang*. But with powerful Western states and a Westernized Eastern state vying with one another in Korea, and affirming that by *their* international law Korea was sovereign and independent, China decided to take steps to protect this dependent member of her family. In keeping with the *shu-pang* status, and not needing to secure any further agreements with Korea, she proceeded to place her own advisers in the spheres of customs and foreign affairs of the Korean government. The reigning Korean monarch was upheld as against revolutionary factions and intervention was used to correct those conditions which might serve as a basis for intrusion by other states.

After 1885 the Confucian relationship weakened as the king of Korea came under the influence of foreigners who urged that he assume the sovereign and independent status legally his. China, therefore, sent Yüan Shih-k'ai as Chinese resident to Korea to direct affairs, particularly in the diplomatic and consular fields. Her early policy of encouraging the foreign states to make treaties of friendship with Korea she also gradually changed to an attempted exclusion of all foreign influence. By 1894, still on the *shu-pang* basis and without the necessity of a legal agreement for each advance made, China had achieved a *de facto* control over Korea which no Western supporter of Korean independence

could deny. It was to overthrow this Chinese position that Japan resorted to war in 1894.

Under the assumption that the *shu-pang* relationship was that of vassal and suzerain, the Westerners, unable to comprehend a subservient relation not based on force, by adroit legal reasoning were able to prove conclusively that Korea was not a vassal, that China was not suzerain, and that Korea was a sovereign and independent state. The logic of this may have been unassailable under Western international law, but to both China and Korea the relationship between them was still that of *shu-pang* despite the Western interpretations of "suzerain" and "vassal." Under the assumption that China had nothing but a religious and ceremonial connection with Korea, Westerners viewed her growing *de facto* control of Korea as pure and unjustified power politics directed against an independent state. Supported by this assumption, Japan was able to end by force the age-old relationship between the two continental states.

When the Sino-Japanese War ended Korea's attempt to be a member of the Western state system and to retain as well the peculiar Confucian relationship to China, Korea became, legally, completely sovereign and independent. Actually, with a habit of subservience to a stronger power extending over centuries, she vacillated between the alternate overlordship of her two strongest neighbors, Russia and Japan. Her independence was merely a diplomatic fiction, since each of these two powers, only to check the designs of the other, loudly asserted its existence. This competition for dominance, plus the Manchurian issues, ended in war between Russia and Japan. The independence of Korea then was paid less lip service, and "paramount interests" became the basis of Japanese policy.

Korea soon went under the protectorship of Japan, first with Japanese advisers in each Korean department of government, and later with actual administration through Japanese officers. The Koreans, who had been amenable to a Confucian relationship with China, naturally chafed under the Westernized control of the Japanese, which was administered with little attempt at conciliation. But the minds of the Korean king and his closest advisers harbored a ray of hope, particularly after the Russo-Japanese War, in a touching belief that under the Treaty of 1882 the United States could be relied upon to save Korea from extinction as an international personality. For, after centuries under a non-legal Confucian elder brother—younger brother relationship, those who ruled Korea had no conception of the limited obligation implied by a treaty guarantee of "good offices." When the king felt the independence of his country threatened by the Japanese, he therefore confidently sought American aid. Rebuffed, he appealed to the international peace conference at The Hague, only to be again refused. This act cost him his throne. Sporadic opposition to the foreign control continued, however, and Japan was forced to use sterner measures. Her first attempt at indirect rule of another nation subsequently ended with the annexation of the nation, and with the adoption of a policy of repression and absorption in dealing with it.

. . . Korea, as the first major step in Japanese expansion, was the stepping stone to the "incident" in China which, in turn, was later broadened into a plan for a "new order" for the entire Pacific. At least on the Asiatic mainland it now appears that Japan was not seeking actual dominium of territory but was rather attempting to re-establish the outward forms of a closed regional international system—a "Middle Kingdom" and surrounding satellites—such as China once headed. Ignoring the legal concept of the sovereignty and juridical equality of states, she set up a group of entities subservient to her will and bound to her by ties which defy accurate legal definition. This system has been called one in which, "instead of the clear-cut lines of jurisdiction and independence so dear to the heart of the usual positivist, is found a condition of legal osmosis with Japanese and Chinese oozing into one another in most shocking fashion." When the past history of the Far East is brought to mind, this "osmosis" is not so shocking, for in this particular aspect, the "new order" was indeed reminiscent of that Confucian system which so confounded the Western visitors of a century ago.

The Japanese-proposed new East Asiatic order lacked, however, the ethical basis which the former Chinese system possessed. Since it was only the Japanese who believed that their emperor was the descendant of the Sun-Goddess and rightful ruler of the world, their control, as a consequence, could be extended and maintained only through force. Furthermore, to use the Confucian patterns and precepts for ruling and at the same time deny them as a guide for rulers, to reject the theory that a ruler governs under Heaven's mandate only so long as he is virtuous, made any revived Far Eastern order of the Japanese a mere façade for the exploitation of the neighboring peoples.

James Crowley

REQUIREMENTS OF NATIONAL SECURITY

To James Crowley (1929–   ), Associate Professor of History at Yale University, traditional militarism is too general a term to explain the creation of Japan's modern army or the origins of Japanese imperialism. Furthermore, parliamentary democracies have also been known to engage in aggressive expansion. The early Meiji leaders were determined to preserve Japan as an independent nation and so naturally concerned themselves with the basic requirements for national security. A modern military establishment required semi-educated conscripts, a trained officer corps, a sophisticated chain of command, strategy and tactics adapted to contemporary conditions, the latest weapons, and sufficient wealth to purchase munitions or preferably an industrial base to manufacture them. For a supposedly militant oligarchy, their initial plans were modest and restrained. Neither was there anything inherently sinister in the establishment of an army general staff, the Imperial Edict for Soldiers and Sailors, the imperial ordinances which stipulated that the war and navy ministers must be active generals or admirals, or the clause in the Constitution which named the emperor as the supreme commander of the armed forces. The original intention was to keep the military out of politics and under control, not to increase their influence. Before condemning Japan, it would be better to learn more about the training and function of the Meiji army and navy and how they arrived at their particular sense of mission. Why, for example, was Korea deemed vital to Japan's security? Then Formosa and Manchuria? Were the bureaucratized samurai really good material for a modern military establishment? Was bushidō more important for its Shinto and Confucian ethical content than for its guidelines to battlefield behavior? It might be well to remember that the notion of war as the pursuit of diplomacy by other means originated, in wording at least, in Western thought. The belief that Japan must be able to defend its national interests in competition with other nations in East Asia was based on sage advice inscribed in Western rulebooks.

READERS of Japanese history are only too aware that amorphous terms—"the Emperor system army," "military cliques," and "militarism"—have been invoked to explain how a "bureaucratic militaristic" oligarchy aborted the development of parliamentary democracy, stabilized the Emperor system of government, and launched Japan into a policy of imperialism. The prevalence of this theme has inevitably precluded serious efforts to comprehend the assimilation of military roles, the primary group structures, the techniques of organizational control, the sense of missions, and the political process by which military policies were resolved during the metamorphosis of the han-samurai armies of Tokugawa Japan into the Army and Navy of Meiji Japan. Indeed, it is still difficult to pass beyond a handful of popular generalities: 1) the kiheitai[1] of Chōshū was the genesis of the

[1] Volunteer militia units of peasants and samurai. [Editor's note.]

From James B. Crowley, "From Closed Door to Empire, The Formation of the Meiji Military Establishment," *Modern Japanese Leadership*, ed. by Bernard S. Silberman and H. D. Harootunian (Tucson: The University of Arizona Press, 1966), pp. 261–262, 267–268, 270–71, 273–282, 284–85.

Imperial Army; 2) French military influence was displaced by Germanic doctrines because of the outcome of the Franco-Prussian War; 3) the "right of supreme command" provided by the Meiji constitution enabled the army to decide such fateful issues as war or peace; 4) the cult of *bushidō* infused the Imperial Army with a "feudalistic" ideology; and 5) the conflicts between the two services were generated by regional interests and motivations, a Chōshū clique ruling the army, Satsuma the navy. The popularity of these beliefs, in turn, justified the contention,

Japan had the form, the external shell of military professionalism, but not the substance . . . for the Japanese . . . the ideal officer was a warrior—a fighter engaged in violence himself rather than a manager directing the employment of violence by others. This was a feudal, not a professional ideal.[2]

In the past few years, the preoccupation with the nefarious consequences of Japanese militarism and of the feudal characteristics of the imperial army has been slowly attenuated by an increasing interest in depicting more precisely the role of the military in the creation of the Meiji state. In harmony with this latest endeavor, this essay offers an interpretative appraisal of the patterns of problems, policies and programs associated with the transformation of the *han-daimyō*-samurai system into the Meiji Military Establishment. In particular, the essay is designed to show how changing definitions or perceptions of "national security" affected the development of the Imperial Army and Navy.

*   *   *

1868–1880: NATIONAL DEFENSE, A
MATTER OF TREATY REVISION AND
A CIVIL ORDER

With the restoration of the shōgunal authority to the Emperor, the immediate national security problem was to "strengthen the country" so that Japan

could conduct its diplomatic relations on a basis of equality with the Western powers. Two steps seemed essential in this quest: an adequate centralized political system and a strong military establishment. During the first two years of Meiji, there seemed to be no serious degree of incompatibility between organizing a strong national army and an effective national government. As Ōmura Masajirō phrased the initial task, "first prepare against civil disturbances, later, prepare against foreign invasion." . . .

*   *   *

Originally the War Department had favored the formation of a large national army, one directed by a well-trained officer corps and capable of great expansion by means of a levy en masse. This vision, however, soon evaporated as the dimensions of the problems became clearer. In Japan, the French military attaché, Albert Charles du Bousquet, cogently outlined the essential requisites for a national army: a professional military educational system, a literate population so that soldiers could be efficiently taught basic military skills, and an industrial base capable of supplying the necessary supplies and equipment. And, General Yamada, [Akiyoshi], after an intensive survey of the military systems in Europe in 187 [2–3], prepared an independent evaluation reinforcing the views of the French attaché. In addition, Yamada stressed the necessity of 1) training a small professional army which could eventually serve as the cadre for a comprehensive conscription army program; and 2) the establishment of a public school system, which would include the rudiments of military training (drill) in the course of study, as the prelude to attempting the implementation of a national conscription program. Yamada's recommendation also embraced another premise, namely, the recruitment of officers theoretically should be open to all citizens.

Obviously, this type of military policy would severely affect the destiny of the samurai. Universal public education would shatter his monopoly of literacy,

[2] Samuel Huntington, *The Soldier and the State* (Cambridge: 1957), p. 126.

an officer corps geared to "men of talent" would deny the premise of samurai military leadership, and a small army would preclude a potential military career for most samurai. The result, thought General Torio Koyata, would be rampant civil disorder plus the concomitant evil of enhancing the danger of foreign intervention. Hence, he countered Yamada's views with the argument that all willing samurai be enlisted in the national army and, after this, the army should be reorganized and trained along Western principles. Despite the creditability of these fears, the majority of the staff of the War Department—Yamagata, Nishi and Yamada—rejected it on two grounds: the government could not afford to equip, feed, and train a force of this size, and there was no imperative strategic necessity for a large army. Hence, the department chose to begin [1872–73] with a very limited conscript program which would provide a national militia capable of preserving civil order.

* * *

1880–1896, THE KOREAN SECURITY QUESTION, THE GENESIS OF A PROFESSIONAL MILITARY ESTABLISHMENT

. . . Throughout the 1870's, the training and philosophy underlying the new army had been derived from the French military mission and a general reading of French military history. Since the immediate task, keeping civil order, placed a premium on practical aspects, there was little opportunity or compulsion to concentrate on strategic planning and the problems of command and administration of a large national army. Rather, the Military Academy taught the skills appropriate to field and company levels of command. In particular, stress was given to the discipline of the troops with a view to cultivating an aggressive combat spirit, the attack *à la outrance* philosophy. Since the War Department was also patterned after the French War Ministry, there was no separate general staff. Thus, when the first significant rebellion flared in Hizen, the govern-

ment appointed the Senior Councilor Ōkubo as Commander-in-Chief of the national army. His deficiencies as a field commander of the new style battalions soon became apparent, along with a perception among government leaders that careful staff planning was as important as the discipline of the new conscripts. Accordingly, serious attention was given to this aspect of military planning. . . .

. . . [T]he basic internal security problem as of 1879 was how to enhance public confidence in the new government. This defined two military tasks: 1) insulating the army from the mushrooming "popular rights" movement; and 2) developing a strong sense of loyalty within the services to the government and its policies. In this context, the army leaders advanced the proposition of utilizing the Imperial institution as the most effective way to promote loyalty within the army. By investing the throne with the "right of supreme command," judged the War Ministry, both officers and enlisted men would become conscious of their personal obligations to serve the Emperor. In turn, ventured Yamagata, this would check the tendency of soldiers to "bewail the times," a trait which could easily lead them into the realm of political activities.

The preoccupation with insulating the army from politics was dramatically illustrated by making the Emperor the commander-in-chief of the army and by the imperial edict of 188[2] which specifically enjoined all members of the armed services to refrain from any type of political associations or activities. While the original motives behind these policies were mixed . . . the principle that professional officers must avoid the domestic political arena quickly became an unquestioned axiom governing the behavior of the officer corps throughout the Meiji era. Without entering into the constitutional aspects of the Emperor's "supreme command" prerogatives, one may safely judge that the Imperial injunction against political action was meticulously cultivated in the officer corps and that this axiom was instrumental in the development of a professional army and navy officer corps. Equally important to the advancement of a professional military elite were: 1) an appreciable increase in the size of the two services, 2) the creation of a complex military educational system, and 3) the acquisition of a sense of mission which both defined the purpose and justified the existence of a strong military establishment in a country no longer suffering from serious manifestations of civil disorder or the prospects of possible foreign intervention. . . . [T]he expanded size of the army [after 1882] plus the inept handling of operations in the Saigō rebellion, had convinced the War Minister . . . that a war college should be organized to train a professional staff. To this end the Japanese government requested the senior Möltke to select one of his most capable staff officers to assist in the organization of a Japanese war college. The following year, 1884, Major Meckel arrived in Japan and introduced a new dimension to the planning and policies of the Japanese officer corps. Without exaggeration, the development of a professional army dates from Meckel's initial lectures at the War College. . . .

A modern army, in Meckel's view, was charged with the duty of securing the security of the nation and of enabling the nation to pursue its national interests in competition with those of other nations. Once a state of war existed, the primacy of diplomacy was replaced by the necessity to wage war in the most effective fashion. Accordingly, the conduct of operations was strictly a military affair, and should be left wholly to the General Staff which possessed the "right of supreme command." But the employment of force was a complex affair. It required meticulous staff and logistical planning, a clear chain of command, and a professional officer corps. To achieve these goals, it was necessary to develop a comprehensive education system which would yield expertise in command, staff and service functions. . . .

In addition to his role in revamping the educational system of the Imperial Army, Major Meckel also furnished a strategic mission which would govern military planning throughout the 1884–1900 period. Surveying the topography of Northeast Asia and the rivalries between Russia and China, Meckel concluded that the "security" of the home islands was contingent upon the "independence" of Korea. No third country, he insisted, should be allowed to assert its control over the Hermit Kingdom, the "dagger at the heart" of Japan. This axiom was soon internalized in the General Staff and the ruling oligarchy, a belief which was reflected in the negotiations with the Ch'ing government between 1883–1885.

At this time, Yüan Shih-k'ai was appointed Resident of Korea and the Chinese sought to reassert their hegemony over the peninsula. In this situation, the General Staff carried out careful logistical estimates concerning possible operations in the Liaotung region, concluding that Japan could not anticipate a successful resolution by forceful means. Confronted with this fact, the government negotiated the Tientsin Treaty of 1885 which theoretically precluded any form of interference in the domestic affairs of Korea by China or Japan. For our purposes, this Korean crisis marked the first instance in which a foreign policy decision was affected by a professional military estimate. It stands in striking contrast to the manner in which the Korean problem of a decade earlier had been decided. Secondly, far more than Meckel's theoretical presentation, the Korean crisis of 1885 set the basic goal of military planning: the development of a military establishment which would be capable of waging war on the continent against the Ch'ing government in defense of the "independence of Korea." Paradoxically, this independence could be secured only by controlling the Liaotung Peninsula, i.e., by compromising the independence of Ch'ing China.

The significance of this strategic mission was reflected in two fundamental ways: It impressed the government and the War Ministry with the necessity to build a fleet which could command control of the China Sea, as well as furnish logistical support sufficient for extensive field operations on the mainland; secondly, it maintained the primary role of the army in matters of national defense. If only because Japan was an insular nation, it is remarkable that the naval aspects of national security remained subordinate to army planning. Yet, the inferior position of the navy was mirrored in its belated development, and in its legal military responsibilities.

. . . Despite the changes of the 1880's, the Naval Ministry was in 1889 entrusted only with responsibility for "matters of coastal defense," and the Army General Staff with matters of "national defense." Moreover, after the creation of the Naval General Staff, the Chief of the Army General Staff was designated as "commander-in-chief of all military forces." Not until the termination of the Sino-Japanese War was this altered so as to make the Chief of the Naval General Staff equal in rank to the Army Chief of Staff.

Ironically, the increasing importance of the Imperial Navy stemmed from the designation of an "independent" Korea as the prime strategic objective. Since this policy had been originally advanced by the War Department, the army naturally based its planning on the inevitability of a war to keep China out of Korea. By 1892, however, naval officers were being "seduced" by the doctrines of Admiral Mahan. Viewing the international scene as a struggle for survival, Mahan reasoned that a large merchant fleet and a strong navy were the requisites for national progress. A country had to trade and cultivate foreign markets, or eventually fall by the seaside. In this picture, trade and commerce, backed by the ability to control the seas, provided the keys to national defense. Since the Korean problem was regarded as a matter of dislodging the influence of any third country from the peninsula, there was at least temporarily no inherent antagonism between the strategic views derived from the doctrines of Admiral Mahan and Major Meckel.

Indeed both services and the cabinet had come to the view by 1890 that an "independent" Japan no longer meant ending the "unequal treaties." Rather, Japan's independence became contingent on its ability to participate in the quest for rights and privileges on the continent. "Within ten years," warned Yamagata, "there will no longer be a Korea or a China but the rule of Three Powers." . . .

1896–1910, CREATION OF AN EMPIRE, TWO STRATEGIC MISSIONS

The war with China had been fought for one main strategic objective, control over the Liaotung Peninsula. A secondary aim, advanced by the Naval leaders, was the acquisition of Taiwan. With this island, Japan could aspire to controlling the sea lanes of the China trade, as well as the southern approach to the home islands. As is well known, the Tripartite Intervention of 1896 by the Powers deprived Japan of the Liaotung Peninsula, but left Taiwan under Japanese control. In addition, Russia promptly extended herself into Liaotung, thereby replacing China as the primary strategic enemy in army planning. By 1898 the Korean problem was no longer a Sino-Japanese affair, but involved the diplomacy of the Powers. No responsible naval officer could envision challenging British sea power; but the Russian position in Manchuria was another matter. If Russia could be isolated from the European Powers in terms of Asian affairs, it might be possible to reassert Japan's position in Liaotung. With this in mind the government in 1896 sanctioned a doubling of the standing army and the imperial fleet. The army was increased to 13 divisions, giving a mobilization potential of 600,000 men; the navy was ordered to construct a 278,000 ton fleet. . . .

Throughout the 1885–1902 period, the "independence" of Korea had provided the starting premise for army policy. Beginning in 1902, however, the Army General Staff concluded that, "for the long-range planning of our country" it was necessary to make "Korea part of the Japanese Empire." While the cabinet did not adopt a similar policy for several years, it seems manifest, in retrospect, that the absorption of the Hermit Kingdom was practically dictated by the nature of European rivalries, especially the advance of Tsarist Russia into South Manchuria and the projected construction of the Trans-Siberian Railway. Dictated, that is, insofar as one accepted the basic Meckelian dictum: the Korean peninsula constituted an inherent strategic threat to the Japanese home islands. Of course, if the Korean state were politically stable, and its sovereignty recognized by the powers, theoretically Japan need not directly establish its authority in order to keep any third power from acquiring the handle of the "dagger at the heart of Japan." . . . That the Imperial Navy had formulated a competing version of national defense policy became evident immediately following the Russo-Japanese War.

In appraising the problem of national defense in 1907, the Naval General Staff argued that Japan was an insular nation with insular possessions. Even the development of overseas trade and commerce, particularly the mainland, was a maritime proposition, as testified by the policies of Britain, France, and the United States. Unexpressed, but implicitly conveyed, was the subsidiary premise that Japan need not inevitably commit itself to any continental acquisition. Japan, in fact, had cornered the Korean market and the world's greatest sea power had, in the 1905 Anglo-Japanese Alliance, confirmed a Japanese hegemony over Korea. The central strategic task, judged Japan's naval planners, centered on establishing naval hegemony over the United States in the Western Pacific. Without this, the United States could entrench itself via the Philippines and pursue its "open door" policy, irrespective of the interests or wishes of the Japanese government. More crucially, without a greatly augmented fleet, Japan's national security would be a phantom, a derivative of the alliance with Great Britain. . . . "In 1907," noted Admiral Fukudome, "the Imperial Navy made the United States its sole strategic enemy."

In a country endowed with greater natural resources and population, the competing views of national defense, the distinctive missions of the army and

navy, might not have been so significant. Still, with the annexation of Korea in 1910, Japan had irrevocably committed itself to a continental (army) and oceanic (navy) role. Its military and naval leaders had defined one comprehensive objective: the maintenance of an establishment capable of meeting the strategic threats posed by the Russian army and the American navy. Within the institutional framework of each service, each strategic axiom was a "rational" or "professional" evaluation. It is a moot question whether the imperial sanction to both views of national defense reflected a comparable phenomenon.

CONCLUSION

*   *   *

. . . [T]hroughout Meiji Japan, military planning and policies always remained subordinate to the decisions of the *Genrō* and cabinet. For example, when the Supreme Command was created in 1893, Yamagata became Chief of the General Staff. Yamagata was not a professionally trained staff officer and, despite the opposition of his staff, he committed the army to the principle of civilian control over such vital issues as the geographical extent of operations and the appropriate time to terminate the hostilities. This precedent was continued during the Russo-Japanese War. . . . If, as Clausewitz declared, war is the furtherance of diplomatic objectives by forceful means, one cannot escape the conclusion that Japan's handling of the Korean and South Manchuria problem during her conflicts with China and Russia mirrored a brilliant coordination of diplomacy and force under astute political leadership. Her conduct of these conflagrations alone belies the clichés that the "right of supreme command" precluded (at least in the Meiji era) viable civilian control over the Imperial Army, and that the Meiji military establishment was "feudalistic" in form, possessing only the "shell of military professionalism." Indeed, throughout the 1853–1910 period, Japan's military policies were invariably distinguished by the primacy of political leadership and political considerations, most noticeably in the clusters of decisions and reforms associated with the demise of the "closed door" and with the quest for an empire within the rules sanctioned by the diplomacy of imperialism. The fascinating fusion of political and martial skills evident in the Meiji Restoration, in the establishment of a national militia, in the creation of the Meiji state, in the development of a modern army and navy, and in the acquisition of an empire, is too consistent to be accidental, too complex to be neatly explained.

Still, one suspects that the genesis of the imperial military establishment and of the Meiji state should be located in the definition of the samurai's mission, initially articulated in the seventeenth century by Hayashi Razan, the official Confucian advisor to Tokugawa Ieyasu:

Teaching the people is a civil act, but warfare is a military act. Without both of them, the people would be thrown away. . . . The Book of Odes says: "Mighty in peace and war is Chi-fu/A pattern to all the peoples." How can a man discharge the duties of his rank and position without combining the peaceful and military arts?

III. NATIONALISM AND EXPANSIONISM

E. Herbert Norman

ULTRANATIONALIST SOCIETIES

The writers in this section all deal with the relation of nationalism to expansionism and aggressive ideologies. Abstractly, modern nationalism may be defined as a sense of shared identity within a single political and cultural entity and a deep pride in distinctive cultural traits. Along the road to such awareness, Japan had to differentiate itself from both China and the West. But in large measure modern Japanese nationalism, to use the phrase of W. W. Rostow, was "reactive nationalism"; it was a consciousness of nation and of the urgent necessity to build a modern state generated at all levels of Japanese society by fear of Western physical domination or cultural colonization. Perhaps for this reason, patriotic pride more readily metamorphosed into ugly chauvinism. In the tortured twists and turns of postrestoration politics, any restrained response by the government to real or alleged threats, or any failure to take opportunities to assert a vigorous policy toward Asian neighbors was denounced as unpatriotic by the opposition whether of a liberal or conservative persuasion.

This phenomenon is discussed in the following excerpts from an article published during World War II by E. Herbert Norman (1909–1957), author of one of the most influential works in English on modern Japanese history, *Japan's Emergence as a Modern State* (1940). Born in Japan of Canadian missionary parents, he received his undergraduate education in Canada and England in the 1930's, completed his doctoral work at Harvard, and entered the Department of External Affairs, Ottawa. He was the Canadian ambassador to Egypt at the time of his death by suicide in Cairo, having previously served as acting permanent delegate to the United Nations and High Commissioner to New Zealand. His friends charge that he was the victim of another form of ultranationalism–American McCarthyism. In 1957, the United States Senate Internal Security Subcommittee was again investigating accusations that he had engaged in communist activities while studying Japanese at Columbia University before World War II, although his government had previously dismissed them.

According to Norman, the Japanese ultranationalists and continental adventurers must not be dismissed as a lunatic group or as crackpots. Over a span of sixty years, from the 1880's to Pearl Harbor, they helped mobilize the nation in support of imperialism. This they did through the propaganda of their nationalist societies, their intelligence network on the continent, their contacts with army officers and big business groups— which may indeed have financed their activities—and through reliance upon violence and terror tactics to persuade stubborn officials. Neither Norman nor later writers, however, have clearly determined how much information they gathered, how accurate and valuable it was, and how closely the adventurers were allied with military and business circles.

From E. Herbert Norman, "The Genyosha: A Study in the Origins of Japanese Imperialism." *Pacific Affairs*, XVII, 3 (1944), pp. 261, 263–70, 273, 278–80, 282–83.

MODERN Japanese politics conform to categories different from those of the West. This does not mean that Japanese politics are so incomparable or opaque that they can resist the analytical scrutiny of a political scientist. But social and economic forces which run parallel to those in Western countries have expressed themselves in Japan in different political forms, whether it be the constitutional development or the role and activities of political parties. One of the most elusive yet characteristic features of political life in Japan since the Restoration of 1868 has been the activities of the so-called "patriotic societies," the prototypes of which are the Genyosha (Dark Ocean Society) and its offshoot, the Kokuryukai (Black Dragon Society). It is difficult to find an adjective or phrase which accurately describes them. They are sometimes termed secret societies but this is misleading since secret societies scarcely publish their own official histories or the biographies of their leading members. Reactionary is at once too broad and negative a term for such dynamic groups as the Genyosha or the Kokuryukai which in the past half century or more have spawned numerous societies concerned primarily with advancing the cause of Japanese imperialism. In order not to be drawn into a too elaborate and perhaps barren theoretical discussion, and for the sake of convenience, these societies will simply be described as "extreme nationalist" or "reactionary," although it should be understood that such terms are merely convenient labels and by no means adequate.

*   *   *

The "Chief of the General Staff" of samurai discontent was Saigo Takamori. His name could kindle the most ardent sentiments among samurai of the whole nation and his exploits even in his lifetime were translated into legend, sure omen of immortalization in future generations. He combined those qualities which made of him not just a natural leader of reactionaries dreaming of a return to the old regime where the war-rior class lorded it over their baser fellows; they made him the very paragon of samurai virtues. In person he was large, of commanding height, powerfully muscled, burly, both a formidable swordsman and a cunning wrestler, a man of immense physical endurance. There was something in him of the swashbuckling brutality and perversion of a Roehm. Displaying the most unquestioning loyalty to the Lord of Satsuma who had twice exiled him at the wish of the Tokugawa authorities, Saigo could be grossly rude to men of finer intellect or higher position whom he found wanting in his particular brand of patriotism. Reckless in battle he was an able general and tactician who took a personal interest in the welfare of the rank and file soldier. He was above all a master conspirator who had been the chief organizer of three *coups d'etat* against the Tokugawa regime, the last of which (November 1867) was brilliantly successful.

After his resignation from the government he returned to his native Kumamoto where he organized the *Shigakko* (Private School).[1] This was regarded as Saigo's own political society where he lectured young samurai of Satsuma on military tactics, but more important he imbued them with his own reactionary views on government, and on the need for Japanese expansion. His chief lieutenant, Kirino Toshiaki, prepared a study calling for the conquest of Korea. The men trained and indoctrinated in the *Shi-gakko* of Saigo were the cadres from which his officers were drawn in the revolt of 1877.

Saigo's personality and his *Shi-gakko* deserve special attention since the most important figures in the later fashioning of Japan's extreme nationalist societies, notably Toyama Mitsuru and Uchida Ryohei, have modeled their characters and political tactics upon the hero of their youth, Saigo Takamori. It was quite fitting then that one of the first official publications of the Kokuryukai under

[1] *Shi-gakko* actually refers to several private schools in Satsuma where ethics and military arts were taught. [Editor's note.]

the editorship of Uchida Ryohei should be an elaborate heavily documented six-volume history of the Satsuma Revolt with rich biographical material on Saigo, his lieutenants and most casual associates. Had he survived, Saigo would have inspired if not organized the type of society which sprang up after his death. Thus in a very real sense Saigo can be called the architect, the first pioneer in the creation of the extreme nationalist societies.

Saigo's fate and later reputation warrant comment in order to throw some light on the official attitude towards the activities of his spiritual descendants. Although a rebel, he has been lauded as the pearl of patriots. His apotheosis has been of incalculable value to the henchmen of Toyama and Uchida whose deeds of violence have been cynically condoned in the Japanese law courts and egregiously praised in the press. The motivation is considered sufficient excuse to absolve them of any stigma of treasonable conspiracy. It should be pointed out that in an official history published by the Black Dragon Society it is stated that Saigo while still a member of the government received warm encouragement from the youthful Emperor on the question of a Korean expedition. Thus the impression was created and has since been strengthened that the Emperor, though separated from such faithful subjects as Saigo by the machinations of self-seeking courtiers or councillors, yet understands and blesses the aspirations of the true patriot —the intransigent expansionist. . . .

The city of Fukuoka in Kyushu is separated from the Asiatic mainland by narrow seas known in Japanese as the *Genkainada*.[2] Fukuoka is the closest Japanese approach to the continent. Today it is the centre of a huge munitions industry, the terminal for air lines linking Japan to the continent and an embarkation point for troops en route to China. It is a city where in recent years few foreigners have been permitted even to alight from the train.

But Fukuoka is more than a strategic centre for the Japanese war machine; it is the spiritual home of the most rabid brand of Japanese nationalism and imperialism. Because of its history and geographical location Fukuoka has been the starting point for all Japanese efforts to secure foothold on the continent, beginning with the semi-legendary invasion of Korea by the Empress Jingo. The district about Fukuoka was the chief target of the Mongol invasions of 1274 and 1281, and it was the main base for Hideyoshi's armadas in his invasions of Korea in 1592 and following years; finally it was the chief base of naval operations during the Russo-Japanese war. In comparatively modern times it has produced more men who have concerned themselves with an aggressive foreign policy than perhaps any other centre. The roster of Fukuoka leaders of expansionist and chauvinist societies is imposing. . . .

In the early Meiji years Fukuoka was a castle-town swarming with declassed and embittered samurai. . . .

In those years small bands of intransigents gathered together in the hostels and tea houses of the old city, declaiming against the government, foreigners, Korea, pension commutation and other targets of reactionary abuse. Some of these groups formed ephemeral societies with such characteristic names as the *Kyoshisha* (Purpose Rectifying Society), the *Kyoninsha* (Stubbornly Enduring Society), the *Kenshisha* (Purpose Hardening Society). . . .

In February 1881 these societies of Fukuoka banded together and formed the Genyosha with Hiraoka Kotaro as its president. . . . The articles of its policy were vague and disclosed nothing of its later history or real nature. Its three principles were to revere the Emperor, to love and respect the nation, to defend the people's rights. In the official history of the Genyosha, it is stated that these broad principles were interpreted to

[2] The Genyosha takes its name (Dark Ocean Society) from this deep gulf separating Kyushu from the mainland. The name signifies its trans-marine or continental ambitions just as the Kokuryukai (Black Dragon Society) indicates the basically anti-Russian orientation of that society since the two Chinese characters for Black Dragon (*Hei Lung*) represent both in Chinese and Japanese the name for the Amur River.

mean that the society would consider itself the guardian of the nation's prestige, ever watchful for slights and insults by the foreign powers. . . .

The leaders in the Genyosha had learned one lesson from the defeat of Saigo. The raising of armed revolt as a means to achieve their goal of a reactionary government at home and expansion abroad was foredoomed to failure. It was not unlike the lesson learned by Hitler from the Munich Putsch of 1923, after which he chose a policy of winning over the key leaders of army, bureaucracy and big business to his program. Henceforth the role of these ex-samurai opposition elements would be primarily to work within the constitutional framework. This did not exclude the use of terror, political blackmail, backstairs intrigue, and other similar favored devices. It simply meant that they would capitalize on a great natural advantage—the profoundly reactionary nature of the bureaucratic personnel, particularly in the General Staff. Thus the Genyosha from the first enjoyed and won many active sympathizers within the state apparatus itself. These sympathizers in the government served as the transmission belt conveying the threats or demands of the reactionary societies to the proper authorities in the government or, at times of great crisis, they would act as go-betweens, personally introducing Toyama or Uchida to some cabinet minister, general or high bureaucrat. In the reverse direction, these contacts in the government kept the leaders of the Genyosha closely informed of government trends and policy.

. . . [F]rom its early days till the present the most forceful leader in it has been Toyama Mitsuru, although he has never formally been named as head of the society. It is appropriate to sketch the character of Toyama, the only surviving and most notorious disciple of Saigo Takamori.[3]

In his early years Toyama appears to have been a reckless youth who despite his poverty was utterly indifferent to

learning a trade or profession. He preferred the turbulent and dissolute atmosphere of the Fukuoka tea-houses and brothels where embittered samurai combined dissipation with sedition. Toyama has retained throughout his life some of the more boorish qualities of the *ronin* without any of that intellectual curiosity and hunger for learning which made some of the *ronin* (masterless samurai) in the late Tokugawa period the first pioneers of Western learning. Toyama never writes for publication but occasionally narrates an incident in his life or some reminiscence of his contemporaries; this memoir is then written up for him by a disciple. His sense of humor, judged even by the most loutish manifestation of Japanese rusticity, is crudely scatological; in his tastes and manners he bears a striking similarity to the "best" Nazi type.

Unlike his boyhood hero, Saigo Takamori, whom he still reveres, Toyama has never displayed that fatalistic disregard for his own life which is popularly believed to be one of the essential ingredients for a leader of *ronin* or "patriots." Perhaps early in his career he came to regard himself as a general who must not lightly risk his life in battle. However that may be, he has been most lavish in sacrificing the lives of his more fanatic disciples not to mention those of his opponents. . . . Like Saigo, however, he has proved a cunning conspirator. In his early career he was often subject to police suspicion for plotting acts of terror in which Genyosha members were implicated, but he was careful never to be found with incriminating evidence. In later years, of course, he has become a law unto himself, far removed from the vulgar considerations of police inquiry. Once secure in his position as "Genro of the *Ronin*,"[4] Toyama's

---

[3] Toyama died in 1944. [Editor's note.]

[4] Genro means "Elder Statesman," the last of whom was Prince Saionji. Toyama is referred to as "Genro of the *Ronin*" in the official histories of the Genyosha and Kokuryukai. *Ronin* (literally, wave-man) in its precise historical sense refers to a samurai who in feudal times was masterless; in modern Japanese usage it means an adventurer, dare-devil, free-lance, etc.

home became a sanctuary for foreign exiles or native terrorists wanted by the police; once within that sanctum anyone is immune against the attentions of the otherwise ubiquitous Japanese police.

*   *   *

Another of Toyama's chief activities has been his sedulous cultivation of Asiatic nationalists and leaders of dissident groups who might be of service in Japanese continental ambitions. It would take us too far afield to relate here the vicissitudes of Toyama's efforts to exploit political exiles, some of whom have been genuine patriots but many again nothing more than potential puppets. Suffice it to give a brief list of the more outstanding figures whom Toyama has befriended. This list begins with Kim Ok-kiun, the Korean revolutionary whose assassination in 1894 in Shanghai spurred Japan's aggressive designs against China; it includes anti-Manchu revolutionaries such as Sun Yat-sen, Huang Hsing, Sung Chiao-jen; prominent Chinese contemporaries such as Generalissimo Chiang Kai-shek and Wang Ching-wei; the Philippine rebel Aguinaldo; the Indian terrorist and present puppet, Ras Behari Bose (to be distinguished from Subhas Chandra Bose, Japan's leading India puppet); the former Russian Moslem leader, Kourbangalieff; the White Russian leader, the Ataman Semyonov; the Afgan, Mahendra Pratap.

Toyama's purpose in extending hospitality to anti-Manchu revolutionaries such as Dr. Sun Yat-sen and his followers was obvious. He hoped that, should they ever take power, they would look to Japan for financial help and advice in the reform and modernization of China, in return granting Japan special privileges, and finally accepting Japanese leadership in all vital matters of domestic and foreign policy. From the others he expected and in many cases received political intelligence; through them the Japanese army and Foreign Office have obtained valuable contacts in such parts of the world as the Philippines, China and Central Asia.

*   *   *

. . . Toyama and his associates were well aware of the close connection between repression at home and aggression abroad. The stifling of free expression, the smashing of all organizations potentially dangerous to a militaristic government were the basic prerequisite for unbridled attacks upon peaceful and helpless neighbors. One of the chief purposes of the Fukuoka Genyosha was the establishment of an unofficial intelligence service by sending young men to China, Central Asia, Siberia and Southeast Asia to collect information on a wide range of subjects. Much of this information would be of value to the army, while commercial and economic intelligence would be of use to the Foreign Office and business houses. Contacts with anti-Manchu secret societies, nationalist groups in colonial territories and dissident Moslems in Central Asia were established and developed. In 1882, Toyama, with the help of the Kumamoto *Soai-sha* (Mutual Love Society) sent over one hundred young men to China to gather information. The most remarkable of these "pioneer patriots in Eastern Asia" was Arao Kiyoshi.

After graduating from the Military Academy, Arao was attached to the General Staff where he became a specialist in Chinese affairs. At his suggestion a special bureau was set up for the study of secret intelligence relating to China; in time it grew into branch bureaus covering all parts of the Far East and Central Asia. Under the instructions of the General Staff he left for Shanghai in 1886 where he set up a branch of the *Rakuzendo* (Hall of Pleasurable Delights) and in the following year moved up to Hankow where he opened another branch.

The *Razukendo* was the creation of one of the most enterprising figures of the late Tokugawa and early Meiji eras, Kishida Ginko. He studied English under Hepburn, the pioneer American missionary, took the manuscript of the famous Hepburn Japanese-English dictionary to Shanghai for publishing, and later was a pioneer in the field of journalism. In 1864 he jointly founded with the better known Joseph Hiko the first Japanese newspaper, the *Shimbunshi*. After a few years in journalism and dabbling in business enterprises with varying success, he entered the pharmaceutical business, not as some petty retail merchant but on a lavish scale, importing not only the medicines and luxury toiletries of the West but also stocking the nostrums, salves and perfumes of the East. His main store on the Ginza was given the happy name of *Rakuzendo*. Anxious to enter the same field of business in China before it was pre-empted by others, he set up branches in Shanghai and Hankow. Kishida had always been interested in the Far Eastern question and was in close touch with societies such as the Genyosha which specialized in the study of China. Shrewdly combining business and "patriotism" he chose his branch managers and salesmen from young men who were either anxious to get a start in the commercial world, or who were pioneers in Japanese intelligence work in China and who could be quite conveniently supported in their work through the proceeds of the *Rakuzendo*. Arao was one of these.

Arao gathered around him in the Hankow *Rakuzendo* a group of young men who made tours into remote parts of Central Asia or China dressed as Chinese with queue and appropriate clothes, speaking the language fluently and supporting themselves by pedding medicines and literature, which consisted chiefly of aphrodisiacs and obscene pictures. . . . The hazards of travel amongst a distant and often hostile people were many. Some were apprehended and detained by Russian police in Turkestan and the leader of one expedition disappeared in Sinkiang without leaving any trace. But all who returned brought with them what must have been the first detailed information available to the Japanese intelligence services on those parts of the world. The chief subjects of investigation included economic and agricultural development; financial conditions and tax grievances; personalities, particularly those likely to be sympathetic to Japan; roads and communications; the Russian, Chinese, Burmese and Indian defenses in Asia, the prospects of utilizing Moslem and Buddhist clergy for Japanese intrigue.

After his work in Hankow, Arao conceived a more ambitious enterprise to push Japanese penetration of China. Returning to Japan in 1889 he resigned his commission as captain, and with the encouragement of Premier Kuroda and Finance Minister Matsukata, toured the country, speaking before chambers of commerce in the larger cities, urging business leaders to enter the China trade. He completed his tour in 1891 and, on the basis of widely circulated applications, he chose one hundred and fifty prospective teachers who were to go to Shanghai to study Chinese language, geography, commerce, finance and related subjects. This school for Japanese agents was known as the *Nisshin Boeki Kenkyujo* (Sino-Japanese Commercial Research). At first this project was impeded by financial difficulties, since promised government subsidies were not forthcoming, but eventually Arao secured adequate financial support chiefly from interested business firms and through Toyama's help. In later years, the number of students increased.

At the end of their course, the graduates of this school were divided into teams of about twenty to make trips into all parts of China, Manchuria, Siam, India, the Philippines, and the South Seas. Later, some would be employed as the local agents of the more enterprising Japanese trading firms; others would enter the Japanese consular service as specialists in Far Eastern trade; many became scouts and official interpreters during the Sino-Japanese war, others again disappeared into the nebulous and ever-growing army of Japanese adventurers whose exact function is hard to define but who have in the course of a half century performed unsavoury tasks for the Japanese army, Foreign Office or expansionist societies.

Arao died in Formosa shortly after the Sino-Japanese war, having performed valuable services for Japanese imperialism. He exemplified in his career the intimate tie-up between Japanese military intelligence, the extreme nationalist societies and business interests, especially those seeking foreign markets.

*　　*　　*

In this description of the origins and development of the Genyosha an attempt has been made to choose for illustration those activities which were most typical and, by drawing the moral from each, to suggest that the scope of these extreme nationalist societies has enormously increased keeping step with the ever bolder and more aggressive plans of Japanese imperialism. A student of Japanese politics who devotes some time to an investigation of these societies must guard, however, against the myopia which comes from scrutinizing at too close range some aspect of Japanese political life, thus exaggerating the importance of one institution or trend at the expense of the totality of Japanese political forces. Thus it would give the reader a false impression if it were implied that Uchida, Toyama and their cohorts were, exclusively and uniquely, the basic driving force behind Japanese facism. But this would be nearer the truth perhaps than the opposite extreme which sees these societies only as the lunatic fringe of Japanese political life, to be dismissed in any serious discussion with a few ironical phrases.

The Genyosha and Kokuryukai . . . and their numerous offshoots have been, for the last sixty years, the advance guard of Japanese imperialism. They have charted the course of aggression and have even thrust themselves into the position of an uninvited pilot who at times of great danger or uncertainty has played a decisive role in guiding Japanese policy along that charted course. It is these societies rather than any political party or succession of parties which have moulded public opinion in favor of aggression. They have provided continuity from one stage to the other in the unfolding strategy of Japanese expansionism. All this has been politically possible only through the unique position which these societies enjoy with regard to the bureaucracy, but more important the army. . ... Utilizing to the full their favored position with regard to the army and bureaucracy, the Genyosha and Kokuryukai succeeded in establishing and maintaining a close but informal alliance with the most ambitious houses, including the *Zaibatsu* (big capitalists), which were interested in expansion as a means of acquiring lucrative overseas markets and a cheap source of raw material. These societies thus are the cement which holds together the whole edifice of Japanese aggression—the army, big business and the key sections of the bureaucracy.

Marius Jansen

PAN-ASIANISM

Many Japanese nationalists were conscious of themselves as Asians who must help other Asians to resist the menace of the white man's imperialism. Asia's only hope was a common effort against the West, and Japan by virtue of its successes in modernization was best equipped for leadership. But should Japan guide by moral suasion, by treaties and alliances, or by force? Professor Marius Jansen (1922–   ) of Princeton University has written extensively on official and unofficial contacts between Japanese and Asian nationalists in the Meiji period and on changing Japanese attitudes toward China. Unlike Norman, who views the relationship as one mainly of deception and exploitation, Jansen perceives in many cases a genuine altruism arising out of a deeply felt sense of kinship with Asians. The continental adventurers were not necessarily forerunners of conquest. Many Japanese sincerely wanted to help Asia, in particular China, revive. Others, of course, mainly those who thought China's prospects for reform were dim, were ready to take advantage of its weakness in the name of self-defense and gain. And there were always those who could not disentangle their desire to help from their desire to dominate. In the following selection, Jansen indicates that the most famous of the Asian revolutionaries, Sun Yat-sen (1866–1925), accepted at face value numerous offers of aid and friendship from Japanese nationalists. Sun's disappointment in official Japan's policies never quite destroyed his belief that the Japanese people were China's friends.

THE conclusion reached by [Meiji] pioneers of commercial and cultural promotion was that China was in a state of temporary degeneration. Her corruption was far less advanced than that of Korea; with Japanese help, China could still be saved from the West. This reasoning . . . received its classical setting from Ōkuma Shigenobu, whose party generally spoke for the commercial interests. The "Ōkuma Doctrine," as the Japanese called it, was set forth in 1898, at the time of maximum imperialist penetration in China. Its essential feature was a *noblesse oblige* whereby Japan, having managed to arrive first at the benefits of Western modernization, guaranteed to China freedom from Western aggression and aid in revamping her governmental system and reforming her social inertia. Ōkuma proclaimed that China would not long remain dormant;

once a hero should arise, patriotism would well up, and China would resume her place among the powers. Japan, a grateful recipient of China's culture and spirit in the past, now promised to repay that debt by holding the West at bay and helping the Chinese hero in his development of a friendly, grateful, China.

*　　*　　*

. . . The Japanese search for a hero who could arouse patriotism and regenerate China for the cause of the Yellow Race led them to Sun Yat-sen. Sun, however, was in many ways an odd choice for that role. He spoke Cantonese, and so he could not converse with the Japanese China experts who had received their training in the Shanghai area. His education was almost entirely Western, and he could not hope to compete with

From Marius Jansen, *The Japanese and Sun Yat-sen* (Cambridge: Harvard University Press, 1954), pp. 53, 59, 202–204, 208–212.

the Japanese who claimed that their values and virtues were based on the traditional classics. Except for a single trip to the northern capital, Sun's knowledge of China was restricted to the Canton area. Therefore he knew less about the land and its problems than many of the Japanese who had spent dangerous years in trips of exploration and reconnaisance. Despite these shortcomings, Sun's character and ability as a revolutionary leader made such an impression on his Japanese friends that they seldom questioned their choice.

The Japanese government leaders were less certain of Sun's attributes. But since he was clearly one of the most important figures among overseas Chinese, the Tokyo leaders assigned contact men to meet and protect Sun. Their money and agents supported Sun in an early project to help Emilio Aguinaldo resist American imperialism in the Philippines. But Tokyo also kept track of the progress of the Chinese Reform Movement of 1898. When this movement failed, the Japanese welcomed reformers and revolutionaries alike to shelter in Japan, and tried to get them together on a united front movement which would deserve full sponsorship. To a Japan which was still not quite sure of its strength and status, and which was still smarting under slights from Western imperialist powers, a union of possible allies was of the greatest importance. Such a union would have solved the thorny problem of which group in China most merited Japanese aid. Moreover, it would also have lessened divisions within Japan.

*   *   *

Sun Yat-sen was central to the whole pattern of Japanese coöperation with the Chinese revolutionaries. When he was in Japan, relations between the two groups were most intimate. When Sun was away, jealousies and doubts replaced friendship and confidence. Of all Sun's followers Wang Ch'ing-wei alone reproduced fully the tendency to look first to Japan for help. It is true that for Sun Yat-sen other help, when it was available, was most welcome, but Western businessmen could never have convinced him so readily of their good will as did their Japanese counterparts. The reasons for this are to be sought in a process of motivation in which Sun Yat-sen's experience was somewhat complementary to that of Japan.

The Japanese rationale for giving help to neighboring revolutionaries . . . derived from both external and internal factors. They were external in that Western imperialism threatened to deprive Asia of all self-determination, and Japan of any economic or political *lebensraum*. They were also internal; a conviction that Japan's tested synthesis of East and West was the surest path to modernization for all Asia blended imperceptibly with historic beliefs of divinity and destiny. This unfortunately rendered most Japanese immune to suggestions of error and deceit, and by the time the militarists had overcome the external dangers there were too few voices raised to protest an extension of the same technique to Asia. Sun Yat-sen and his cause were then unceremoniously discarded for more direct and more promising means. In this process, the Japanese alienated most Chinese. It should be stressed, however, that the break with Sun Yat-sen himself was never so complete as to remove the possibility of a reconciliation. . . . What, then, were the sources of Sun's reluctance to think ill of his Japanese benefactors?

Like the Japanese, Sun's attitude derived psychological support from external and internal factors. Externally, Japanese imperialism never affected him as directly and as critically as did Western imperialism. Except for his release from the Chinese Legation in London in 1896 and his brief flurry of popularity and respectability in 1911, Sun Yat-sen had bitter and increasingly acrimonious relations with the official channels of the Western governments. These altercations at times hindered his plans, as did the British refusal to let him land at Hong Kong in 1900; at times they affected him personally, as when the Portuguese revoked his permit to practice medicine at Macao in 1893, and at other times, as in the Shanghai community's reception of him in 1924, they infuriated him. Despite Sun's cordial relations with and sincere affection for many individual westerners, those men were never able to persuade their governments or parties to commit themselves to Sun's causes. Moreover, as Japanese imperialism became more obvious and more dangerous, Sun's relations with the West grew increasingly tenuous. These factors played an important part in his continued reluctance to think the worst of his second homeland.

Internally, Sun's actions derived from a sense of destiny only slightly less intense than that of his chosen allies. The conviction of consecration to the task of liberating China that came upon Sun in his London prison in 1896 never left him. Despite the many dagger men available to the Manchus and to Yuan Shih-k'ai, Sun never doubted for a minute that he would be spared to finish his proper task. In his sense of security, the charismatic charm that won him support and sanctuary so often must have played an important though unconscious role.

Sun's sense of destiny naturally bred the conviction that what was good for him was also in the best interests of China. Once he was able to associate the fate of China with his personal lot, the various compromises and adjustments he made with Japan and the Japanese could all be interpreted to China's gain. By an understandable corollary, what was bad for Sun's enemies was good for China. Thus the many obvious Japanese moves against the Manchus and against Yuah Shih-k'ai could seem merited by the recipients and, curiously, advantageous for the broader aims of the Chinese revolution.

All these assumptions then reinforced Sun's acceptance of the Pan-Asian ideas of his Japanese friends. That acceptance, however, went through several periods of emphasis and nuances of meaning.

*   *   *

[After the Revolution of 1911 and during World War I] Sun Yat-sen became less idealistic, increasingly disillusioned, and far more bitterly resentful of British imperialism than ever before. The sordid struggles for position and power of the warlords kept China in constant turmoil. Sun's political organizations featured an increasingly rigid central control. In his thinking, the period of "party tutelage" which should precede "democracy" loomed ever more important. The young idealist who had organized the project to help Aguinaldo in 1899 could now refer to the wisdom of America's decision to educate and civilize the Filipinos before giving them self-rule.

When Sun tried to show the way by establishing a "model" regime at Canton, he was repeatedly the victim of his own political ineptness and inability to work constructively with others as equals. What disturbed him most, however, was the discovery that he was to be greatly limited by British control over the Canton customs receipts. His dislike for the Western imperialists hardened. To the denizens of the Treaty Ports he came to seem a virtual Bolshevik. In 1923 and 1924 Canton merchants organized to subvert Sun's plans for the reorganization of the city. Sun, fearing another setback, put them down at the cost of considerable fighting and destruction. At the same time, Sun's new relations with Russia drew Western fire. Sun had changed his mind about Russian imperialism since the advent of the Soviets, and from 1923 on he was in increasingly close touch with advisers who aided and superintended the reorganization of the Kuomintang. Western business circles, who had seen in Sun's struggle with the Canton merchants proof of his radicalism, found their worst fears confirmed by his new alliance.

. . . [Later, 1921–23] Sun won new favor among a younger student generation which had organized in response to foreign insults. During the Canton customs difficulties, Sun's vigorous anti-British statements had helped increase his stature among those students. To be sure, after the Versailles settlement Sun also issued several strong statements against Japanese policy. Nevertheless, his bias against the West remained too strong to admit a forthright anti-Japanese stand. . . .

Sun's last major address was delivered to a large audience in the Kobe Prefectural Girls School on November 28, 1924. He took as his subject Pan-Asianism. . . .

Sun's speech was, in the main, a restatement of his beliefs about the basic superiority of Asian culture and virtues. He pointed out that Asia was the source of the world's civilization, and that the Greek and Roman civilizations had been transmitted from Asia. Despite Asia's historic role, however, it had grown weaker at the very time that Europe had gained in strength. As a result a steady decline had set in for all Asian nations. Out of this decline they had been newly awakened by the rise to independence of Japan: "the day when the unequal treaties were abolished by Japan was a day of regeneration for all Asiatic peoples." Japan's victory over Russia had indebted Asia further to her. "We regarded that Russian defeat by Japan as the defeat of the West by the East."

Sun then turned his attention to westerners who considered the rising of the East as a revolt against civilization. He refuted them by pointing out that Western civilization was based upon scientific materialism which resulted in a rule of force. This cult of Might was far inferior to the Oriental culture which was based on virtues of benevolence, justice, and morality—the Kingly Way. The problem of Pan-Asianism was a cultural problem of the conflict of the Occidental rule of Might with the Oriental rule of Right. There was, for Sun, no question of their intrinsic strength. Nepal, for instance, had sent tributary missions for centuries to China of her own volition. But if England should fall, all her contact with Nepal would cease overnight.

Benevolence alone, however, would not conquer the West; Asia was indebted to its two sentinels, Japan and Turkey, who had armed themselves. Similar measures should also be taken by China. Together with those progressive forces in Western countries that had begun to see the primacy of benevolence, Asian arms would then ensure Asian liberation. Already, progressive forces were to be found in most Western nations; one entire country had already reoriented her policy to insist on the rule of right and advocate the principles of benevolence and justice. For this reason, Russia was now being shunned by Europe. She had subscribed to the Oriental values.

Sun's final words were addressed to his hosts of the evening:

We advocate the avenging of the wrong done to those in revolt against the civilization of the rule of Might, with the aim of seeking a civilization of peace and equality and the emancipation of all races. Japan today has become acquainted with Western civilization of the rule of Might, but retains the characteristics of the Oriental civilization of the rule of Right. Now the question remains whether Japan will be the hawk of the Western civilization of the rule of Might or the tower of strength of the Orient. This is the choice which lies before the people of Japan.

It was primarily in this speech that Wang Ching-wei claimed to find the justification for his coöperation with Japan.[1] The Japanese felt that it constituted a fitting conclusion to Sun Yat-sen's years of friendship with them. . . .

Actually, the speech was not the blanket endorsement of Japanese policies that Wang made it seem. But it is clear that at the end of his life Sun Yat-sen was still not convinced that Japan had chosen a course unfavorable to China. And if Sun, at that late date, was still so reluctant to abandon the dream of his revolutionary years, it is evident that during the Meiji Period those ideas and ideals of Asiatic coöperation were more than the contrivance of Japanese imagination. They represented a reasonable and probable solution to a very present problem, and they were abandoned only gradually and reluctantly as the Chinese revolutionaries saw Japan try to justify a rule of Might with Oriental maxims of Right.

[1] Many years later, after the Japanese invasion of 1937. [Editor's note.]

Matsumoto Sannosuke

NATIONAL MISSION

Japanese national pride found expression in a sense of mission just as nineteenth-century American nationalism was reflected in the spirit of manifest destiny. In this selection, Professor Matsumoto Sannosuke (1925–   ), a specialist in Japanese political thought and nationalism who teaches at the Tokyo University of Education, is concerned with the formation of Japan's sense of mission and its special characteristics. He uses the thought of two famous Pan-Asianists, Okakura Kakuzō and Tokutomi Sohō, to illustrate the increasing absorption of Japanese intellectuals during and after the Sino-Japanese War in the question of Japan's role in East Asia and the world. In part because certain of their ideas were incorporated into the propaganda of the 1930's, both of these men, once held in high esteem, are now very much out of favor; but there is no denying the significance of their thought. Okakura (1862–1913), better known by his pen name Tenshin (Heavenly Heart), gained fame as an art historian, a museum curator (including a stint as director of the East Asian Collection in the Boston Museum of Fine Arts), and a founder and director of art schools. Along with Ernest Fenollosa, an American teacher in the employ of the Japanese government, he helped redirect attention to the glories of Japan's traditional art and architecture and the duty to preserve and protect them, rather than toss them out on the ashheap of history as a sacrifice to progress. In his books, written originally in florid English prose and later translated into Japanese, he affirmed his love for Asia and those things which Japan shared with Asia: unity in diversity, pacific Buddhism, and cooperative socialism. Japan, it was true, had risen to its present greatness through Westernization, but its primary claim to greatness was its ability to retain the essence of the old while incorporating the best of the new. While learning from the West, Japan had retained its unique character–its spiritual self which was born in Asia. There was no Japan without Asia and no modern Japan without the traditional Japanese spirit. Tenshin's sense of kinship thus transcended geography and race and drew upon the realm of spirit and culture. He would have Japan help Asians wipe out the shame of Western domination by inspiring them to a self-awakening and a sense of pride. It was his fate, says Matsumoto, to be remembered for his attacks on white imperialism but not his strictures against force and exploitation.

The views of Tokutomi Sohō (or Iichirō, 1863–1957) were far less romantic and emotional. One of modern Japan's most prolific journalists and writers of popular history, he received various high awards from the government for his services to the state. By his own testimony, the great event in his young life and the one which converted him from democracy and pacifism to power politics was Japan's loss of the Liaotung Peninsula through the triple intervention in 1895. However, says Matsumoto, his writings at the outbreak of the war reveal that he had already begun to argue with a great deal of pride that the Japanese people were expan-

From Matsumoto Sannosuke, "Kokuminteki shimeikan rekishiteki hankan" (Changing Views of National Mission), *Kindai Nihon shisōshi kōza* (Studies in Modern Japanese Thought), VIII (Tokyo: Chikuma Shobō, 1961), pp. 83–90, 92–98, 100–08. The editor is responsible for the translation but owes a debt of gratitude to Shinkawa Kensaburō and Tsai Tuh-sun. Tenshin's prose is his inimitable own, having been written originally in English.

sionist by nature. He saw war with China as a good opportunity to express this fundamental urge to expand. Japan's mission was to extend its political organization throughout East Asia and the South Seas as a benevolent gift and to create a *Pax Japonica*. In the process Japan would save the rest of Asia from white imperialism.

I. THE MAIN THEME

. . . Concepts of national mission did not become an important theme in Japanese thought until after the Sino-Japanese war. Japan had of course resumed relations with the outside world, in particular the West, at the end of the Tokugawa period. In those early days, views on Japan's mission in the world were, as we know, naive but nevertheless loudly voiced. A good example would be the ambitious call of Yokoi Shōnan (1809–69): "We should follow the way of Yao, Shun, and Confucius and learn what we can from the machine technology of the West. Why should we stop at enriching our country and strengthening our army? It is our supreme duty to spread righteousness throughout the world." However, Japan's basic problem at that time was how to create a national state. As we all remember, it was urgent that Japan establish an independent and unified nation, one which could "stand side by side with all of the foreign countries" and "rank equally with the Powers." Japan simply had not yet arrived at the stage where it could discuss such an active and positive attitude toward the world as a national mission. Quite the contrary. Japan's problem was how to form a nation capable of bearing such a mission. . . .

Japan's intellectual energies were therefore concentrated almost exclusively on internal reconstruction, but in due course there came a turning point. Japan's victory over China, commonly regarded as the great country of East Asia, was attributed to the extraordinary efforts made since the Meiji Restoration to achieve wealth and power. As a new and rising country, Japan was at last able to gain self-confidence and feel assured of its independence. . . . As Tokutomi Sohō wrote in December, 1894: "This war against China certainly marks a new epoch in our history. It has forced

us to make the leap from national life into world life." As he further explained, "Thirty years ago, the Japanese were aware only of what happened in their own domains. Now we are concerned about the life of the entire nation. In the future we must pay attention to the whole world. Our ambitions and plans should be conceived on a world scale" ("The True Meaning of the War against China"). According to Sohō, this expansion in the range of vision of the Japanese people from domain and nation to the world should be seen as a progression from regionalism and nationalism to imperialism. . . .

. . . When Japan further raised its status in international politics by defeating Russia in 1905, the question of national mission became even more serious. As Sohō expressed it, if the Sino-Japanese war marked "the period when the Japanese people became conscious of their imperialist power," then the Russo-Japanese war marked "the period when the world recognized Japan as an imperialist power" ("Youth of the Taishō era and the Future of the Empire"). In short, Meiji Japan had become literally Japan in the world. . . .

Representative of this new emphasis was the journalism of Miyake Setsurei (1860–1945), who addressed the opening words of his newly renamed magazine *Nihon oyobi Nihonjin,* January, 1907, to "my dear fellow countrymen and *brothers and sisters of the whole world*" (italics added by the author) and proclaimed: "The idea that the world is composed only of white people, that all new inventions and new designs are the monopoly of white people, that God rewards only those who love and worship the saint of Judea and condemns the rest, all these ideas have undergone considerable change as a result of the recent war, have they not?" . . . From this time until the fascist period of the 1930's, there were repeated references to the Russo-Japanese war in propaganda about the national mission. The war was indeed a milestone in such thought. What specific attitudes and views were expressed as a result of these two wars?

II. "ASIA IS ONE"—ON OKAKURA TENSHIN

. . . The need to reexamine the process of Westernization had already been brought to the attention of the public in the mid-1880's, a good ten years before the Sino-Japanese war. For example, preservation of the national essence was promoted by Shiga Shigetaka (1863–1927), Miyake Setsurei, and others in the magazine *Nihonjin,* the organ of the Political and Education Society. There was also the nationalist thought of the journalist Kuga Katsunan, editor of the newspaper *Nihon.* However, the intention of these nationalist movements was merely to counter blind admiration for Western institutions and culture or temper their indiscriminate introduction and not to criticize "Westernization" itself. They wanted rational adoption of Western civilization in accordance with Japan's actual needs (taking whatever is good to supplement our shortcomings). Underlying them was recognition of Japan's backwardness but also deep anxiety about superficial, unhealthy Westernization. In contrast, the national self-awakening after the Sino-Japanese war, being infused with feelings of conceit and satisfaction stemming in large part from the victory, fostered a positive, self-assertive manner in confronting Western civilization of the sort not found in the earlier nationalism and national essence movements. . . .

Japan's self-recognition now took two basic forms. Here I will use two leading thinkers to illustrate these trends: Okakura Tenshin and Tokutomi Sohō. As is well known, both men were prominent in shaping and advocating views of national mission after the Sino-Japanese war when there was mounting national self-awareness. To both, the problem of the time was how to urge the people of Japan and East Asia to end the subordinate position imposed on them by Europeans. However, they had diametrically

opposite views on the role Japan should play in Asia and in the world. Briefly, Tenshin's thought was rooted in aesthetic romanticism. Sohō's displayed recognition of the realities of power. I would first like to examine in some detail the position of Tenshin.

According to Tenshin, the construction of modern Japan was a "twofold problem." The first was "accomplishing the national unity," and the other was "building up the military against Western conquest" (*Awakening of the East,* 1902).[1] In other words, this twofold problem was "the Asiatic ideal" and "European science" (*Ideals of the East,* July, 1903). He saw the formation of the spirit and culture of modern Japan as the history of conflict between these two elements.

There are today two mighty chains of forces which enthral the Japanese mind, entwining dragon-like upon their own coils, each struggling to become sole master of the jewel of life; both lost now and again in an ocean of ferment. One is the Asiatic ideal, replete with grand visions of the universal sweeping through the concrete and particular, and the other European science, with her organized culture, armed in all its array of differentiated knowledge and keen with the edge of competitive energy. (*Ideals of the East*).

Of these "two mighty forces," it was obvious that beginning with the Meiji Restoration "European science" and "European institutions and civilization" had exerted an overwhelming influence on Japan. In order to cope with the "white disaster," that is the "Western invasion" or "the glory of Europe," Japan had to sharpen the "sword," that is adopt "the policy of strengthening the army and navy." As Tenshin further explained, "It is brutal strength that they can understand and respect" (*Awakening of the East*). Therefore, even though Westernization had resulted in extensive destruction of Japan's traditional culture, Tenshin was somewhat sympathetic to

[1] *Awakening of the East* was written in 1902, after a trip to India, but published posthumously in 1940. The other dates refer to the actual time of publication. [Editor's note].

the position of the Meiji statesmen that "no sacrifice was too great to bear to enable Japan to compete ably with others in the new contest." And he was willing to admit that Japan had been able to obtain "a position among the modern powers" by following this policy (*Ideals of the East*).

However, Tenshin did not agree with those who saw the glory of Japan in its having been first in Asia to modernize and acquire equal standing with the Western powers. If Japan had anything to boast of, it was the "assimilative power" which had allowed it to adopt Western civilization without losing the unique character of its tradition, or the "maturity of judgment which made her select from various sources those elements of contemporary European civilization she required" (*Ideals of the East*). To what did Japan owe its assimilative power and maturity of judgment? Let us listen again to Tenshin.

Our sympathizers have been pleased to marvel at the facility with which we have introduced Western science and industries, constitutional government, and the organization necessary for carrying on a gigantic war. They forget that the strength of the movement which brought Japan to her present position is due not less to the *innate virility* which has enabled her to assimilate the teachings of a foreign civilization than to her capability of adopting its methods. With a race, as with the individual, it is not the accumulation of extraneous knowledge, but the realization of the self within, that constitutes true progress. (*Awakening of Japan*, November, 1904; italics added by the author).

... Moreover, said Tenshin, Japan's "self-within" was born and nurtured in the geographically and historically unified cultural area of Asia. Therefore Asia was the only "true source of our inspiration," and without Asia the existence of Japan was inconceivable (*Awakening of Japan*).

Now, what in fact did he mean when he said that Asia was the mother of Japan? The answer can be inferred from his teaching on Asian unity, as revealed for example in his famous slogan "Asia

is one." In what did Tenshin see oneness? He argued:

Asia is one. The Himalayas divide, only to accentuate, two mighty civilizations, the Chinese with its communism of Confucius and the Indian with its individualism of the Vedas. But not even the snowy barriers can interrupt for one moment that broad expanse of love for the Ultimate and Universal. . . . (*Ideals of the East*).

He believed that love for the ultimate and universal was "the common thought inheritance of every Asiatic race" and penetrated the differences between the Chinese and Indian civilizations. Because of this, Asia transcended national differences and was in essence a single entity.

*   *   *

. . . He criticized the Western concept of freedom and personal rights as "that crude notion," as "that perpetual elbowing through the crowd." And he saw the Western family as "a duet of man and wife," in contrast to the spirit of the "Eastern idea" of a family collectivity based on "the triad of father, mother, and child." According to him, the eastern family

involved at once the triple relations of paternal care, marital helpfulness and filial obedience, bound together in indissoluble bonds of mutual loves and duties, which when widened into the social ideal, flower into that Benevolence, Brotherhood, Loyalty and Courtesy which constitute the beauty and fragrance of Asian life. The Western dualism was never completely merged in the family ideal, for the individual asserted itself even there, just as in the social system, where it never ceased to be the fundamental unit. The protests of selfish rights and the demarcation of personal property blur connubial felicity, and form the source of those incessant discords and unfortunate failings, so distressing to our eyes. (*Awakening of the East*).

. . . Since Tenshin always praised the internal beauty and morality of Asian culture above that of Europe, it was natural for him to attribute Japan's early achievements in modernization to its Asian spirit and not to "westernization." . . . Yet he warned: "Woe to the people that have no external foes, for they have no occasion to reorganize themselves" (*Awakening of the East*). An "external foe" was the chief stimulus to "the awakening of the East." However, and this is important, he saw Asia's self-awakening and self-assertion as ultimately sustained by its spiritual culture, such as the traditional philosophy, art, religion, and morality, rather than supported by might. "The military never held that pre-eminence in the Orient that they assumed in the West." This was the case even in Japan, he argued, for the major duty of the samurai was not in "sharpening the blade" but rather in "polishing the mirror of the soul." . . .

It is apparent from what has been said up to now that Tenshin's view of national mission rested on two main points: the essential unity of Asia and the leadership of Japan. In modern Japanese thought there is nothing novel in the notions of kinship with Asia or Japan as the leading nation of the East. However, in most cases, identification with Asia has been based on geography and race, that is on the sense of a common fate, and has not been a deeply-felt conviction rising out of the depth of the soul. . . . Certain concepts of oneness with Asia were in actuality the product of great contempt and deep distrust of other Asian countries as primitive and provincial. . . . Feelings of kinship in combination with a sense of superiority formed the basis of Japan's view of Asia for a long time. This double-edged view . . . made it seem natural for Japan to be the "leader" in Asia but also deluded Japan into extending self-righteous *control* over Asia in the name of "kinship" and "guidance."

Tenshin's sense of oneness with Asia, in contrast to the usual feelings, was distinguished by an intense subjective attachment. For Tenshin, the kinship of Japan with Asia was the meeting of soul with soul. The two were tied together by a common spirit as found in their art, religion, and philosophy. So personal a

view as this denied at the very foundation any feelings of contempt or sense of difference, such as those contained in the common saying that Japan is "civilized" and Asia "primitive." . . .

Therefore, Japan's mission in Asia was not that of "civilization" leading and controlling "the primitive" but rather of stimulating the self-awakening of Asia. "The brilliant resurrection of Japan is very instructive as an instance of Asiatic revival," he said (*Awakening of the East*). Since Japan had preserved from ancient times the ideals of Asia, had experienced in itself the unity of Asia, had awakened early to the spirit of Asia, and most of all had achieved its revival while facing the storm of the "white disaster," Tenshin did not deny that it should play a leading role in Asia.

The Chinese war, which revealed our supremacy in the Eastern waters, and which as yet draws us closer than ever in mutual friendship, was a natural outgrowth of the new national vigor, which has been working to express itself for a century and a half. It has also been foreseen in all its bearings by the remarkable insight of the older statesmen of the period, and arouses us now to the grand problems and responsibilities which await us as the new Asiatic Power. Not only to return to our own past ideals, but also to feel and revivify the dormant life of the old Asiatic unity, becomes our mission. (*Ideals of the East*).

Japan's mission was thus the reconstruction of Asia. And since Japan's own reconstruction had been the result of "self-awakening," made possible through the "realization of Japan's internal self," the reconstruction of Asia similarly required that Asian countries should awaken to themselves. . . . The implication was that Japan must set limits on its external assistance and guidance, even though offered with the best of intentions and sympathy. The role of leader required supreme intelligence and strict self control. Tenshin in fact called for such qualities: "Each Asian nation must seek within itself the seed of its regeneration. The Pan-Asiatic Alliance is itself an immense force, but the individual factors must first feel their own strength. The slightest reliance on foreign assistance, however friendly or sympathetic, is an unpardonable weakness and unworthy of the Great Cause we are to inaugurate and accomplish" (*Awakening of the East*). As is well known, it was Tenshin's fate to be exhumed in later years by fascist propagandists as the sage and prophet of the "New Order in Greater East Asia." His intelligence and discipline had vanished without trace in the currents of that time. Only his impassioned voice calling for the unity of Asia and resistance against the "white disaster," was left. Why was this so? To answer that, we will have to look at Tokutomi Sohō, a contemporary of Tenshin who also had considerable influence in shaping views on Japan's mission.

III. "AN EXPANSIONIST NATION"— ABOUT TOKUTOMI SOHŌ

"If the Meiji Renovation was the time of Japan's national awakening, it would not be an exaggeration to say that the Sino-Japanese war was the time of Japan's imperialist awakening. After two turbulent decades we Japanese had *just begun* to know ourselves. To know ourselves was to know our power. It was to know our mission." So wrote Sohō in "The Youth of the Taishō Era and the Future of the Empire" (November, 1916). To be precise, we should say that this was how Tokutomi Sohō as an individual Japanese explained the change in his own thinking as a result of the Sino-Japanese war. His ideas about the nation were at two levels, which should carefully be distinguished from each other. One level reflected the development in national thought and the other his own ideological transformation.

*   *   *

By Sohō's own later admission, his change in outlook was caused by the shock of Japan's having to return the Liaotung Peninsula to China after the triple intervention. He wrote: "Up to that time, I had learned from books. The Sino-Japanese war taught me a lesson from reality. This was of course not the first time I had learned from actual events, but the war did exert a profound and lasting influence on me. It had an even greater impact on me than the thought of Spencer, Cobden, Bright, and the others. Obviously what I am referring to is the retrocession of the Liaotung Peninsula" (foreword to "My Personal View of Current Affairs," November, 1913). What was this "profound and lasting influence"? We can sum it up in just a few words, "the gospel of power." "I was baptized in the gospel of power," he said, "by the triple intervention." To Sohō, who had been taught to believe that "reason is the master— where reason directs, all follow," the Liaotung retrocession was "a vivid lesson in how reason was completely defeated by unreason." To quote from his autobiography, "It would not be too much to say that the retrocession of the Liaotung peninsula altered the course of my life. After hearing the news, my whole point of view changed and I became almost a different man." (*The Autobiography of Sohō*).

This was what Sohō remembered. There may be some truth in saying that his reaction to the retrocession was *one* of the factors in his conversion to nationalism and imperialism only ten years after he had made his initial mark in journalism by advocating democracy and pacifism. But it is doubtful whether his words "After hearing the news, my whole point of view changed and I became almost a different man" tell the whole truth. If we examine his statements, one by one, before and after the Sino-Japanese war, we will find that Sohō recalled only part of the story. After the war, in reply to public denunciation of him as "an apostate," he stated in an article sent to Yamaji Aizan:

It is all too obvious that my opinion has progressed from pacifism to imperialism. But it should be remembered that my conversion is closely related to the following two facts: first, the change in Japan's international standing after the Sino-Japanese war, and second, the trend throughout the world toward imperialism. As early as the end of 1894, I wrote "An Essay on the Expansion of Greater Japan" and advocated imperialism. At that time, no one thought of me as an "apostate" for those views. And not only that, some influential journalists even made similar proposals, if not exactly echoing my appeal. Now I am called an apostate because I have been consistent in my thinking while those progressive gentlemen enjoy the reputation of being righteous and virtuous simply because they were skillful in adjusting to changes in public opinion ("Society and the Individual," September, 1899).

Here Sohō openly admitted that his change in thinking was caused by the Sino-Japanese war; yet he made no allusion to the triple intervention. Furthermore, Sohō even stated that he had already advocated imperialism as early as 1894, in his essay on expansion. Actually this was a collection of articles he had written for the journal *Kokumin no Tomo* and the newspaper *Kokumin Shimbun* from June, 1894—just before the outbreak of the war—to the end of that year. He would later refer to it in his memoirs as a "living witness" to his conversion to imperialism. As the title implies, Sohō wrote that the "salvation of the Japanese people" lay in progressing from "a shrinking Japan" to an "expanding Japan." We should note that although *in reality* his argument had originated unmistakably in the existing tension between China and Japan, he did *not* advocate "national expansion" in the *logical sense* that war between the two countries was likely to occur and expansion was a means to achieve Japan's war aims. He advocated expansion for its own sake. He believed that "contact with the outside world and progress" had been "national policies ever since the founding of the nation," and considered population growth and adaptability to changes in climate to be evidence of expansionist traits inherent in the special character of the Japanese people. In the preface to his essay, he had stated: "Seventy to eighty per cent of my argument is related to the problem of the war with China. But I do not regard the expansion of greater Japan as the problem of the war against China. On the contrary, I regard the war against China as the problem of greater Japan's

expansion. That is, Japan's expansion is the precondition of the war against China and not the other way around." Sohō's words are very revealing. Believing that "expansion is the precondition of war," he did not advocate expansion *only for the purpose of* war with China. The war was simply "a golden opportunity" that Japan, whose natural destiny *was* to expand, had come across *by chance*. That was Sohō's logic. For example:

A golden opportunity is difficult to come by and easy to miss. Now, it is about to kiss us, to shake hands with us. I do not know yet how the politicians of our government are going to react. What is meant by a golden opportunity? It means a chance to wage war on China. In other words, this is a golden opportunity for expansionist Japan to engage in expansionist activities ("A Golden Opportunity," July 23, 1894).

. . . This admiration for expansion inevitably led Sohō to glorify the vigorous spiritual energy which nurtured the power to expand. Such qualities as a tough vitality which enabled the Japanese people to adjust to severe cold and extreme heat, a "steady and persevering spirit" which endured hardships and privations, and a "patriotic" selfless devotion to country which motivated the "sacrifice of individual life to public life" were all singled out and praised by him as the national characteristics of "expansionist Japan" . . . ("Plain Living and High Ideals," June 1895). . . . After the Sino-Japanese war, Sohō boasted that, among other lessons, it taught that "the country which combines primitive vitality with a knowledge of civilization is the greatest power in the world" ("The Primitive Spirit and Knowledge of Civilization," July 1895). In his opinion, there were "evils in civilization and advantages in primitivism." Japan had won because "its spirit of eastern vitality allowed it to make the most of its knowledge of European civilization." Such was Sohō's conceit as a Japanese. . . .

Thus at a time when the fundamental issue in Japanese thought had come to be Japan's role in the world, Sohō saw

Japan as "expansionist Japan," that is he viewed the special character of the Japanese people as "expansionist." It would not be an exaggeration to say that this interpretation decisively stamped his view of national mission, a view strikingly different from Tenshin's. . . . To Sohō, "national expansion" was rooted in the history and national character of Japan. It was an "inevitable tendency" and "destiny." It was the highest ideal in the natural order and should direct the ultimate aims of state action. Expansion abroad was *kokutai* or national essence, and therefore as sacrosanct as rule by the emperor in domestic affairs. In Tenshin's view, Japan's mission was to preserve Asian civilization and inspire other Asian peoples to a self-awakening, but to Sohō, Japan's essential mission was "to demonstrate its expansionist character." He said:

Upon careful consideration of the destiny of the empire of greater Japan, I realize that it bears a special mission. What is that mission? To spread the benefits of its political organization throughout the Eastern world and the south seas. If we make comparisons with the past, isn't Japan's mission in modern history the same as Rome's mission in ancient history? ("Romans and Japanese," July 1895).

. . . To use Sohō's favorite words, Japan's mission was "to spread righteousness throughout the world." He meant that it was "our duty to guide backward countries to the point of being able to govern themselves" and "to maintain peace in East Asia for that purpose" ("The Meaning of an Independent Foreign Policy," February 1898). He also meant that Japan should aim at "the destruction of the white man's privileges in the world" ("On Viewing the Opening of Japan from the Perspective of History," February, 1896). Sohō's view of Japan's mission in Asia was inseparable from his belief in Japanese *political* superiority in Asia. . . . On this point, he said that "today in East Asia only the Japanese have the competence for political organization. Only the Japanese people are conscious of nation. . . ." Sohō added that "it is reason and the power to back reason which lend strength to the statements of diplomats. If we advocate humanity and justice but lack the power to practice them, then we are indulging in empty talk" ("The Meaning of an Independent Foreign Policy"). And "benevolence without the power to support it is just like a cannon without any shells. It may make a big noise, but in fact it can't have any effect, no matter how loud it sounds when fired. . . . If I am not mistaken in my reasoning, benevolence means that the powerful make good use of their power" ("Good Use of Power," April 1904).

In these opinions of Sohō, there is nothing sufficiently brilliant or penetrating to dignify with the name of national mission. It is also difficult to find any serious moral worth in them. They are merely an expression of "realism" and unworthy of a "national prophet" who ought to explain history and mission as the conscience of the people. . . .

Although Sohō outgrew his infatuation with Western learning, he did retain the image of a unified world under the rule of universal principles, which he had gained from his studies of western civilization. He acknowledged that "Japan is a part of world society" and that "differences in religions and races should not be a wall against humanity" ("World Citizen," 1902). . . . As Sohō indicated when he compared the Japanese to the ancient Romans, he expected Japan to be an apostle of "universal civilization." He wanted it "to create a great equal society for the benefit of the world and to perform its mission with the intention of furthering the progress of humanity and civilization" ("On Seeing the Opening of Our Country from the Perspective of History"). . . .

So we see that Sohō's view of national mission was based on two concepts: "expansionist nation" and "world citizen." . . . As his confidence in Japan's "real power" increased, his consciousness of "Japan in the world" and his pride in Japan as a participant in "universal civilization" were also gradually intensified. But the attitude of international society toward Japan was not necessarily satisfactory. As he pointed out: "The

Japanese were previously considered superior to black peoples but inferior to Chinese. Now that has changed, and the Japanese are regarded as superior to the Chinese. But we should not be content until we have been recognized as equal to the white race" ("By-products of the Russo-Japanese War," May 1904). The white race's "ideal of universal brotherhood" had not yet been extended to Japan, and there was still reason "to fear that Japan would be regarded as an outsider." This condition existed because Western countries "had not yet attained a proper understanding of the true essence of universal civilization." Such being the case, Sohō assigned to Japan, a lonely and proud apostle of "civilization," the difficult dual mission not only of "enlightening and guiding Asian countries" but also of "awakening Western countries." As he put it: "When I analyze and examine the mission of our empire in the future, I am led to conclude that it is more important for us to awaken the West than to spread Western civilization in the East" ("Japan in East Asia and in the World," June, 1904).

IV. THE ECONOMIC ARGUMENT

O. Tanin and E. Yohan

CAPITALISM AND EXPANSIONISM

Imperialism, caution many writers, must not be too narrowly defined as the extension of political control overseas, for it also includes various forms of economic dominion. Accordingly many questions have been raised about the economic roots of Meiji expansionism and the relationship between empire and modern economic growth. It is said that the profit motive, not patriotism or nationalism, fueled the drive for empire. More complex is the orthodox Marxist-Leninist argument that imperialism is the final stage of monopoly or finance capitalism. In this interpretation, the Sino-Japanese and Russo-Japanese wars must take on the coloration of imperialist wars even though Japanese capitalism at that time was not very advanced. Such a view is presented below by two Russian scholars, Tanin and Yohan, whose work appeared in English translation in 1934 and about whom little else is known. Basic to their argument is the analysis of the Meiji Restoration as an incomplete revolution. A centralized state was created from above by the more progressive feudal elements. Initially, the Meiji leaders had to rely on the financial support of a narrow base of merchants but moved quickly to encourage the growth of industrial capitalism while preserving feudal conditions in agriculture. All this was to the advantage of merchant capitalists, landowners, and bankers but harmful to the peasants. Without a social revolution, Japan was doomed to political absolutism and the expansion which inevitably accompanies it. Tanin and Yohan concede that Japan's aggression before 1894 was not an expression of monopoly capitalism, then scarcely in existence, but an effort to satisfy the young industrial sector which looked abroad to overcome the handicap of a backward domestic economy. Since internal markets were small, the Japanese bourgeoisie wanted and needed empire along with state subsidies and other forms of assistance in order to complete the fundamental task of capital accumulation. Between 1894 and 1904 the interests of the bourgeoisie merged with the strategic concerns of the generals, reinforcing the long-standing territorial ambitions of military circles and resulting in an alliance of the capitalist and feudal classes for foreign conquest. By the time of the Russo-Japanese war, Japan had embarked upon the initial phase of true finance capitalism and would, therefore, more systematically rob its neighbors to sustain its own economic growth.

THE new government, which continued the policy of concession to the foreigners begun by the Shogunate, was looked upon by the nationalistic circles of the former Samurai as a force which was incapable of defending the national interests of Japan. The Samurai believed that it was their destiny to further the extension of Japan's influence on the continent and in the South Sea Islands, and thus increase her strength and power of resistance to the "white race,"

From O. Tanin and E. Yohan, *Militarism and Fascism in Japan* (New York: International Publishers Co., Inc., 1934), pp. 28, 30–31, 36–43.

i.e., the United States, tsarist Russia, England, and France. These circles did not see the salvation of Japan in the adoption of European civilization and European institutions, thus attaining the same level of development as the "white race." The government tried to do this, but it was hopeless: "While we are taking one step forward, they leap far ahead." "Only by means of an active foreign policy and of expanding on the continent of Asia," asserted these circles, "can the country emancipate herself, and not by means of Europeanization and internal reforms."

... Such were the vague and undefined sentiments of the lower strata of the Samurai, who identified their caste interests with the interests of the whole nation.

*   *   *

... It must be borne in mind that the government possessed very few resources [1868–1894] for satisfying the demands of the Samurai, for fulfilling, in particular, the demand of the opposition Samurai for an active foreign policy of conquest. Under such circumstances, it was difficult, therefore, in spite of the government's policy of concession, to achieve reconciliation with the Samurai opposition. In view of the fact that Japan herself was a semi-colony of the great capitalist powers, her possibilities of external aggression were naturally very limited. Most of her expeditions of conquest ended in a fiasco, and only served as pretexts for new accusations against the government of feebleness, indecision, capitulation to the foreigners, and so on, and consequently, for investing the Samurai opposition with new vigor.

*   *   *

... When the Japanese attempted to seize Formosa in 1874 in order to appease the Samurai opposition, Great Britain made them return Formosa to China. But by the middle of the 'nineties the situation had changed. The desire to seize new colonies had grown very strong in England by this time, while at the same time signs of future complications in Asia began to loom on the horizon, and threatened to become serious obstacles for the aims of British policy. First of all, tsarist Russia and the United States had become very strong on the shores of the Pacific Ocean, and a new imperialist competitor, Germany, had made its appearance; secondly, the situation in China was becoming such that there was a threat of the repetition in the very near future of the Taiping rebellion on a new, higher basis.

This complication of the situation in Asia, which was taking place at a time when the hands of the British were tied in other parts of the world, forced England to seek allies in Asia itself. Japan, which had already set out on the road of European reorganization and thirsted for military exploits, could be utilized for this purpose. England decided to conclude a conditional agreement with Japan, which would take effect a few years later if Japan fulfilled the obligations she had undertaken. As is well known, the war between Japan and China started a fortnight after the signing of the Anglo-Japanese agreement of 1894.[1] It is also well known that among the concessions which Japan obtained from China by the Treaty of Shimonoseki, were such points as the opening to foreigners of a number of ports in the basin of the Upper Yangtze, in which the Japanese had very little interest at that time but which were of great importance to the English; included in the treaty was the right of foreigners to open up *industrial concerns in China*, in which also the Japanese were as yet uninterested, but for which the English had long been fighting.

Although the Anglo-Japanese Alliance was formally concluded only in 1902, these facts are sufficient to show that the war between Japan and China was on Japan's side not only a method of strengthening herself for her own national emancipation struggle by robbing her neighbors, but it was also a direct inclusion of Japan in the ranks of those

---

[1] A reference to Japan's first equal treaty with a Western power. [Editor's note.]

rapacious powers who looked upon China "as a prey to be torn asunder by the Japanese, the English, the Germans, etc." (Lenin). In exchange for these services Japan obtained from the English in 1899 the Anglo-Japanese agreement on the abolition of consular jurisdiction, which was followed by similar agreements with other countries.[2] By participating in 1900 in the suppression of the Boxer rising in China, Japan definitely demonstrated her competence to participate in imperialist alliances. The years 1904 and 1905 (her victory over tsarist Russia) made this fact unquestionable. We can therefore agree with Haushofer when he says:

If in 1895 the war between Japan and China gave Japan the importance of a great power on a limited area, if participation in 1900 in the Boxer expedition gave Japan the possibility of forming alliances beyond the frontiers of Asia—the victory over Russia in 1905 gave Japan the importance of a world power.[3]

As a result of the war between Japan and China, the aggressive and imperialist tendencies within Japan itself gained enormous strength.

This evolution can be understood in connection with the processes that were going on in the economic structure of Japan. For only those processes can explain it fully, and reveal what social functions were being fulfilled in that period by Japanese aggression on the continent, and whose interest organizations of the Black Ocean type were serving in this connection. Its very first steps showed the Japanese bourgeoisie to be a good ally of the feudal Samurai military caste. To the militarist fervor of the Japanese generals the bourgeoisie added its readiness for conquest as a means of increasing the rate of primitive capitalist accumulation, which was hindered by the small capacity of the internal markets of Japan. But if this need for seizing more and more colonies became

later an absolute necessity for the Japanese bourgeoisie, it was not only because "its appetite grew while it ate," or because it was bound to its semi-feudal allies, but because, after the ten-year period which lay between the Japanese-Chinese war and the Russo-Japanese war, Japanese capital speedily began to take on a new form and entered the new, imperialist, stage of its development.

It would, however, be wrong to consider, as some authors do, that the transition of the Japanese bourgeoisie in close coöperation with the military-feudal bureaucracy (and we may add, under the political leadership of the latter) to an active policy of conquest on the continent can from the very first steps of this aggression be explained by the entrance of Japanese capitalism into the phase of *finance capital,* and that the further extensive development of Japanese colonial aggression can be explained entirely by the needs of finance capital and large-scale monopoly industry.

In the ten years which lay between the Japanese-Chinese war and the Russo-Japanese war . . . Japanese capitalism had not yet acquired the characteristic features of the epoch of finance capital. And moreover, it was not based on anything like a solid foundation of large-scale industry. It must not be forgotten that even six years after the war between Japan and China (in 1900), of the 7,171 industrial enterprises in Japan, only 2,388 employed mechanical power, and that the total power of the prime movers in Japanese industry scarcely amounted to 90,000 h.p. Even in 1903 the value of imports of raw materials and manufactured articles into Japan was nearly double that of Japanese exports. . . . The war between Japan and China, thanks to the 350,000,000 yen indemnity received from China, the opening up of new Chinese markets, the manufacture of war materials, and so on, greatly stimulated the accumulation of capital and the rapid industrial development of Japan. Nevertheless, from the above figures we have seen that even six years after the Treaty of Shimonoseki, *i.e.,* on the eve of the Russo-

[2] What actually happened was that the agreement made in 1894 went into effect. [Editor's note.]
[3] K. Haushofer, *Japan und die Japaner* (Berlin, 1923) p. 120.

Japanese War, Japanese capitalism, relatively to capitalism in other countries, had attained a very low degree of development. At the same time it is highly important to point out that of the 7,171 industrial concerns which existed in 1900, 4,150 were in the textile industry, and that this was the only industry which had made progress (it already possessed nearly a million spindles) in comparison with other branches of industry.

What, then, explains this desire for colonial expansion on the part of the Japanese bourgeoisie in the 'nineties of the last century and the first years of this century? *Not the high degree of development of Japanese industry, nor the fact that modern finance capital had already come into existence in the country, but the extreme backwardness of every other branch of Japanese national economy and the whole class structure of the country,* which hindered the development of Japanese industry, insignificant as it was, within Japan, and caused the development of Japanese capitalism to take an *outward,* and not an *inward* direction. To a certain extent what Lenin wrote about Russian capitalism of the 'nineties can be applied to Japanese capitalism of this period:

The expansion of the home market is hindered by many factors (chiefly by the maintenance of obsolete institutions which retard the development of capitalism in agriculture), and the manufacturers are not, of course, going to wait until the other branches of national economy attain the level of capitalist development in the textile industry. The manufacturers are in urgent need of markets, and if the backwardness of other branches of national economy narrows the market in the old district, they will seek a market in another district or in other countries or in the colonies of the old country.

As the compromise agreed upon with the feudal lords did not permit the Japanese bourgeoisie to destroy the medieval structure of husbandry (as a matter of fact, the bourgeoisie itself soon became territorialized, *i.e.,* connected with the feudal landownership), it continued to *adapt* itself to this structure and

found a means, in new colonial seizures, of reducing the sharpness of the contradictions between the rapidly growing large-scale industry and the preservation of feudal relics in the whole national economy of the country.

The solution of the contradictions characteristic of, and generated by, capitalism is temporarily set aside, owing to the fact that capitalism can easily develop in width (Lenin). The search for a way of "developing in width" was the reason why the Japanese bourgeoisie set out so early on the path of colonial expansion. Later (approximately beginning with the period of the Russo-Japanese war), the progress made by Japanese national economy was so great and was of such importance that it is permissible to speak of the entry of Japanese capitalism into the phase of finance capital. But even then . . . it was not the pure form of finance capital.

Thus when we say that the period of struggle for national emancipation in Japan and the period of colonial expansion not only lay very close to each other, but actually overlapped, these phenomena in the sphere of politics are closely connected with parallel processes in the sphere of economics—are, in fact, based on them. However, as it often happens at certain stages politics run ahead of economics, but only in order that the tendencies which had already made themselves apparent in economics should develop all the more fully and rapidly.

Here it is important to note, however, that the years 1894–1904 were the turning point in the policy of the ruling classes of Japan. It was these ten years that saw the beginnings of the aggressive military-feudal type, which later became fully realized in material form, of Japanese imperialism.

But it was this, however, which decreased the urgency and sharpness of the contradictions both between the bourgeois parties and the government, and between the "patriotic" movement and the government. The bourgeoisie—in spite of the fact that later (in 1906–1908) its contradictions with the landowners grew sharp over the questions of agricultural taxes, bread prices and car-tel prices of industrial commodities—nevertheless took the line of recognition of the inviolability of the compromise with the feudal lords, and the recognition and support of the military monarchy whose sword had cleared a way for Japanese capital on the continent. Thus there was no necessity to oppose constitutional slogans to the clan government and monarchical bureaucracy, and the process of political coalescence between the organizations of the bourgeoisie and the landowners was hastened. The bourgeois-landowning political parties, in spite of all their mutual wrangling, became a perfectly acceptable means of cooperation between capital, semi-feudal landownership, and the military and police monarchy which crowned this system. The period of "the struggle for the constitution" became a thing of the past. The "constitution" of 1889 was a worthy result in material form of this union between the classes.

. . . This does not mean that there were no conflicts and discussions over the directions to be taken by this aggression, its rate, the nearest enemies, etc. Some groups among the ruling classes inclined more towards Central and South China and the Pacific Islands, *i.e.*, towards markets and regions of raw material for *light* industry, and consequently raised the question of ascendancy on the sea and the inevitability of a struggle against the United States. Others sought a *rapprochement* with the United States and endeavored to direct Japanese aggression towards northwest China, *i.e.*, towards sources of fuel and minerals for *heavy* industry. The War Ministry was inclined to support the second group, while the Naval Ministry supported the first group. These differences were of very ancient [*sic*] date, and originated in fact at the beginning of the twentieth century, when Marshal Yamagata was for forming an alliance with England and preparing for a war with Russia; while Ito considered it imperative to enter into an alliance with Russia and to expand along the Pacific Ocean. But in any case, after the Russo-Japanese War the domination of southern Manchuria and the Kwangtung region proved to be of advantage not only to heavy industry, but to light industry as well; in addition, it was accompanied by the gradual expansion of influence in Central China (although before the World War expansion met with very stubborn resistance on the part of the great imperialist powers), which brought in huge profits to light industry and navigation. . . .

The most important characteristic of Japanese imperialism is precisely the fact that it never did pass through the stage of industrial capitalism in the same manner as western Europe or the United States. In the narrow frame of the decade between the Japanese-Chinese War and Russo-Japanese War were squeezed the solution of the problems of primitive capitalist accumulation, the creation of a rough industrial basis for Japanese capitalism, and the preparation for the transition to the epoch of finance capital and imperialist policy. This transition was already taking shape on the basis of the victory of the Russo-Japanese War, and that parallel process of internal reorganization of Japanese capitalism was taking place which was leading it into the stage of finance capital. Where was there room for the development of the "liberalism of the epoch of industrial capital?"

Fujii Shōichi

CAPITALISM, INTERNATIONAL POLITICS

AND THE EMPEROR SYSTEM

Japanese historians have engaged in furious battles over the true nature and significance of the Sino-Japanese and Russo-Japanese wars, in particular over the relevance of the economic motive. It is much like the clash among American historians over the Spanish-American war and the background of America's rise to world power. Representative of a popular view in this debate is the work of Fujii Shōichi (1921–   ), professor at Ritsumeikan University in Kyoto and a former student of the well-known Marxist historian Inoue Kiyoshi of Kyoto University.

Fujii has considerably refined the preceding arguments of Tanin and Yohan although he has essentially the same approach. He accepts Lenin's thesis that imperialism is the dying stage of the capitalist system but adds that this is an abstract statement with serious limitations. If we allow only economic logic, how do we explain that Japan with a small capitalist sector in 1894–95 was nevertheless clearly imperialist? We must look carefully at the specific historical context. Fujii, therefore, makes the international scene and the politics of the emperor system as important as economics. The Sino-Japanese war was the first large-scale aggressive war in modern times. It gave impetus to capitalism but was itself caused more by the lingering predatory ambitions of generals and bureaucrats than by the economic designs of the bourgeoisie. In the long run, of course, Japan's empire could not have been built without the driving force of the capitalists. After the China war, Japan gave far more attention to promoting overseas trade and investment and accelerating domestic industrial development. In competing with Western interests in East Asia, Japan compensated for its lack of surplus capital by its proximity to the Asian continent and military power. This was the age when Western imperialism threatened the whole world, and naturally the international politics of imperialism directly influenced Japan's foreign policy. In Fujii's analysis, the turning point was Japan's decision in the summer of 1900 to send troops to China in cooperation with the allied powers in an effort to quell the Boxer Uprising. With this act, Japan joined the Western powers, the white race, against the Chinese peasants, the yellow race, thereby showing its true imperialist colors.

Fujii would be the first to admit that his general statements might need revision on the basis of new findings. His argument is straightforward, but he does employ a few technical terms. Indeed his article is of interest not only for its contents but also for its Marxist phraseology and logic. By political merchants, he means those who were able to obtain government aid through right connections in high places–for example, the Mitsubishi and Mitsui enterprises. By parasitic landlords, he refers to absentee landowners who exploited the peasants by charging high rents while paying only moderately high taxes. They might be former daimyo,

From Fujii Shōichi, "Teikokushugi no seiritsu no Nichi-Ro sensō" (The Emergence of Imperialism and the Russo-Japanese War), in *Jidai kubunjō no rironteki shomondai* (Various Theoretical Problems in Historical Periodization), ed. by Rekishigaku Kenkyūkai (Tokyo: Iwanami Shoten, 1956), pp. 45–50, 52–59. Translation and paraphrases by the editor, with the assistance of Shinkawa Kensaburō.

samurai, wealthy farmers, or merchants. By emperor system, he goes beyond Tanin and Yohan's military monarchy to designate a special kind of political absolutism, the essential feature of which was a theoretically all-powerful and semi-divine emperor who in fact was under the control of bureaucrats in alliance with bourgeoisie and landlords. Together they resisted the demands of workers and peasants and cynically promoted orthodox teachings on the mystic union of people and emperor.

I. THE PROBLEM—EXPLAINING THE IMPERIALISM OF BACKWARD COUNTRIES

. . . From an economic point of view, imperialism is, as Lenin says, monopoly capitalism, but I think it is also a *historical* phenomenon with considerable political substance and meaning. As I explain later, for example, there were remnants of semi-feudal relations in Japanese agriculture at the end of the nineteenth century. Within capitalist enterprises too, backward elements lived together with the new in a symbiotic state. Under such conditions, no matter how much progress there was in Japan's industrial revolution by the end of the century, I do not think we can argue in purely economic terms that Japanese capitalism had reached the stage of imperialism. Although we use imperialism as a general term, it in fact has characteristics which are shaped by different historical conditions. . . . Japanese imperialism emerged as a problem in the years from 1900 to 1902, and its character was clearly feudal, militarist, and dependent. . . .

II. THE EMERGENCE AND CHARACTER OF PREMATURE MONOPOLY CAPITALISM

When we discuss the problem of the emergence of Japanese imperialism, we must ask before anything else what stage of development Japanese capitalism had reached [commercial, industrial, financial, or parasitic and perishing]. I would therefore first like to touch upon the development and nature of Japanese capitalism with the Sino-Japanese war as a turning point. Modern Japan undertook its first large-scale war of aggression, the Sino-Japanese war, at the end of the nineteenth century. There are numerous opinions on the nature of

that war, and the controversy still rages. If we consider the stage of Japanese capitalist development at that time, I think we could say that the Sino-Japanese war was caused by the traditional ambition of the emperor system for territorial acquisition, now greatly reinforced by the emergence of industrial capitalism in which primary capital accumulation was nearing completion. The objective significance of the war was to set the stage for colonial exploitation whose chief design in turn was further primary capital accumulation.

As the victor, Japan was able to force an unequal treaty on China while still suffering itself from similar unequal treaties previously imposed by European powers and to destroy completely China's political and military supremacy in Korea. Furthermore, through enormous wartime profits, extortion of reparations from China, and acquisition of extensive territories and markets, Japan's industrial capitalism made rapid advances. Strategic industries were promoted by the government, and huge capitalist enterprises operated by political merchants were beginning to dominate the economy. . . .

Japanese capitalism had remained in the industrial stage until the Sino-Japanese war, and there was virtually no export of capital overseas. However, victory together with rapid development in banking and finance, allowed Japan to establish the basis at least of a distinctively Japanese premature monopoly capitalism. What made this premature growth possible? Big capital, the accumulation of which was the result of government favoritism and the demand for military equipment, acquired profits by paying industrial workers extremely low wages and absorbing the small deposits of farmers in special agricultural and industrial banks and industrial cooperatives, thus taking advantage of the relative overpopulation of rural areas. All of this was possible because of the firm support provided by the absolute political system. In Japan's case, monopoly capitalism did not emerge under the same conditions as it had in the advanced countries of the West. . . . Most Japanese industries which produced goods for sale in competition with the products of advanced capitalist powers in domestic and foreign markets came to be managed in such monopoly forms as the trust and cartel early in the Japanese industrial revolution. At the very top, there were four great *zaibatsu* [financial cliques], that is monopoly organizations: Mitsui, Mitsubishi, Sumitomo, and Yasuda. Thus Japanese capitalism, which had taken the form of political-business monopolies in the first years of the nineteenth century, was already beginning to evolve into monopoly finance capitalism at the turn of the century.

However, semi-feudal relations of production were still very pronounced in agriculture, and wages were extremely low in urban industries, with capital concentrated in the hands of a few. As a result, the consuming power of the mass of workers was relatively low and the domestic markets were narrow. Big industries were necessarily forced to expand into foreign markets and make strong demands for access to overseas materials and resources. Since there were some areas in Korea and China which were relatively difficult for the imperialist powers of Europe and the United States to penetrate, Japanese capitalism had great advantages in its proximity to the continent. In order to secure these areas as its colonial market, however, Japanese capitalism could not avoid a decisive struggle with other imperialist powers. I will discuss this later.

The tremendous importance of the continental market to Japanese capitalism is very clear from the following memorial submitted by representatives of the Tokyo Association of Commerce and Industry to the minister of foreign affairs in September, 1895, immediately after the Sino-Japanese war.

After considering the possibilities of an import-export trade with Manchuria, we believe that the most important product they can sell us is beans. We could also import their soy beans, bean cakes, soybean oil, cocoons of wild silkworms, and furs. The most important thing we can sell them is cotton goods. We could also export cotton yarn, sugar, silk goods, iron products, and matches, among other things. Since the demand for these products is now considerable, if a port were opened now on the southeastern coast of Manchuria, we would enjoy easy access to the market. Obviously mutual trade would expand steadily through that port.

As I have already indicated, when we look at the actual development of capitalism in Japan before World War I, the power of financial capital was still rather weak although its monopoly character was exceedingly strong. Of course, the enormous concentration of government capital was helpful in compensating for this deficiency, but the point to be stressed is that the economic foundation of Japan as an imperialist power remained inadequate. That is to say, Japanese capitalism did estabish an imperialist system but not as a result of distinct changes in the economic structure. It was the very weakness and inner contradictions of this capitalism that forced Japan to appear in the world arena as a premature imperialist power. Even before Japan had fully established monopoly finance capitalism in its basic economic structure, while it was in fact still consolidating its premature imperialistic aggression and domestic power structure as a member of the imperialist powers of the world, its capitalist imperialism was bolstered by two advantages: the concentration of power in the hands of the military, who operated within the pyramidal structure of the emperor system, and geographical proximity to the continent, which facilitated the monopoly of profits from trade with neighboring countries. Furthermore, it was the inner contradiction of Japan's imperialism to be armed by an unusual militarism and very much dependent upon and subordinate to the imperialism of other powers. . . .

III. INTERNATIONAL FACTORS INFLUENCING THE EMERGENCE OF JAPANESE IMPERIALISM

. . . The most important event in international relations which conditioned the emergence of Japanese imperialism was the Boxer Uprising in 1900. This peasant revolt which broke out in great ferocity all over China at the turn of the century was of great significance for two reasons: It was the first resistance of the yellow race against white imperialism in Asia, and it led to the final division of the world by the imperialist powers or the beginning of the period of world wide imperialism.

China's defeat in the war with Japan had opened it to aggression by the world imperialist powers and intensified their mutual antagonism, which up to this point had been mainly concerned with the area to the West of India. . . . Russian czarism, beginning with the triple intervention, played the principal part in the competition among the imperialist powers to divide China. . . . As a backward country, Russia suffered from a narrow domestic market and had experienced the urge to expand as early as the 1870's. This urge was a natural expression of the aggressive character of czarism. Consequently the expansion of Russia inevitably assumed a highly militaristic and aggressive character. The target of Russia's advance shifted from the Near East (Turkey) to East Asia. . . . To meet the demands of the Russian governing class for new markets in East Asia and improved trade routes, it was necessary to construct the Trans-Siberian Railway and shorten the route to those markets in favor of Russian capital. Construction was begun with the support of French capital in 1891 after the conclusion of the Franco-Russian alliance. In due time, trains began to arrive at a steady pace in East Asia carrying in their freight cars the thievish interests of the Romanovs and those of the Russian industrial bourgeoisie and French financial capital.

*   *   *

At the turn of the century, as the division of China continued, the great powers changed from a policy of encroaching upon China's frontier regions to the acquisition of coastal and interior areas having great economic and strategic importance. Under the pretext of "leaseholds" the powers forced China to cede her economic and strategic centers semipermanently, and, moreover, in most cases, the powers also acquired railway concessions and the right to cut timber and exploit mines along the railway lines. . . .

At this point there occurred the great event which marked, as already mentioned, the establishment of world wide imperialism: the Boxer Uprising or the first large scale racial resistance of Asians against imperialism. After the Taiping Rebellion in the middle of the nineteenth century, peasant revolts had erupted intermittently in China for several decades. They grew more intense, expanding in scale and increasing in number in the 1890's, particularly after the Sino-Japanese war. The insatiable appetite of the powers—the threat of the "division of China"—provoked rapid social upheaval, especially in the region of North China where the invasion of the imperial powers had destroyed agriculture and domestic industries. With economic depression added to this in 1898 and 1899, the rural areas were in desperate straits. Faced with these social conditions, groups of peasants rebelled in every part of China. . . . Among them, the I-ho chüan [the Boxers], whose parent organization the White Lotus Sect had jolted the power of the Ch'ing dynasty even before the Opium war, commanded the largest following and rose up in violent peasant revolt when Germany attempted to construct a railroad and land troops in Shantung province. The Boxer Uprising was spontaneous, but the eight powers of England, Germany, France, Italy, Japan, Russia, the United States, and Austria organized an allied expedition to suppress this large-scale, anti-imperialist, racial resistance. . . .

This was Japan's golden opportunity to participate in international intervention. With the intention of securing, if possible, the strongest voice among the imperialist powers and the biggest share in the spoils, Japan dispatched 12,000 troops, the largest contingent in the total expedition of 23,000 troops, and joined the imperialist war for the open division of China. How Japan attempted to use this opportunity to gain hegemony among the powers is revealed in the following opinions which Komuro Jutarō, the Japanese minister to Russia, submitted to Aoki Shūzō, Minister of Foreign Affairs, before and after the dispatch of troops.

Our country must always have a military and naval force equal at least to the strongest power in China so that we will not be left out of the united European group at the time of the final solution of the incident (June 26, 1900).

The total number of Russian troops in China will soon reach more than 20,000. . . . It is advisable for our imperial government to dispatch quickly those divisions which have already been mobilized, for it is imperative that we maintain a balance of power in the number of troops (June 29, 1900).

Russia and other European powers have stated their views on the methods required to meet the pressing problems of the day. I believe that our country will be able to gain in influence in relation to the European allies if we make the best of this opportunity in China and take quick and firm action in the spirit of complete cooperation with the powers (July 12, 1900).

In these statements, we see how carefully Japan weighed the probable aims and reactions of the powers and what it hoped to gain by participating in this imperialist expedition with 12,000 troops. And so, at the sacrifice of China, Japan was able to secure for the first time the status of a powerful nation and to acquire the international role of "the policeman of East Asia." The Anglo-

Japanese Alliance of 1902 further strengthened this position.

Although the imperialist powers had been able to cooperate in united action to invade and divide China, as soon as the incident was ended, antagonism and contradictions appeared again among them. Russia, which had loudly opposed Japan's "independent dispatch of troops" and "freedom of action," now itself resorted to independent military maneuvers and steadily pursued a policy of monopolizing Manchuria, using the Boxer Uprising as a pretext. England began to feel uneasy about this turn of events. In addition, antagonism surfaced between England and Germany when the latter supported Russia's East Asian policy. Germany's intention was to further intensify antagonism between Russia and England and to ease its own advance into the Near East by weakening the force of the Franco-Russian Alliance against itself. Therefore, East Asia at this time was the focus of world attention. England, challenged not only by Russia but also by France and Germany, was forced to give up its policy of "splendid isolation" and seek allies. Consequently, the Anglo-Japanese Alliance was concluded on January 31, 1902, for the ostensible reason of maintaining the status quo and general peace in East Asia, in particular the territorial integrity of China and Korea and the policy of the open door.

Having England as an ally, Japan was now in a position to protest with confidence Russia's East Asian policy. For its part, England hoped to rely on the Japanese navy, considerably expanded since the Sino-Japanese war, both to check the advance of the powers toward India and to maintain its commercial and other interests in China against Russian designs. Japan also wanted to carry out an imperialist policy of developing continental markets in competition with Russia's steady penetration of Manchuria and Korea. After the conclusion of the Anglo-Japanese Alliance, the possibility of war breaking out between Japan and Russia depended very much on the international situation just described, that is on the reality of contradictions and antagonisms in the system of world imperialism.

Although Japanese capitalism in those days had not yet reached the point of monopoly finance capitalism, we must concede that Japan was rapidly elevating itself to the stage of imperialism. Because of its capitalist nature, Japan could not, of course, retreat to any degree under the pressure of the advanced powers nor look on with indifference at the imperialist division of the world. Japanese participation in the Boxer incident truly meant the door to eminence for Japanese capitalism as "the policeman of East Asia." With the conclusion of the Anglo-Japanese Alliance in 1902, Japan took its first ambitious step into the actual battlefield of imperialism as a faithful but opportunistic assistant of the most powerful imperialist nation in the world. . . . Japanese imperialism was thus dependent in the sense that it was able to plunder Asian countries but still required the financial and diplomatic assistance of the great powers. . . .

IV. THE CONSOLIDATION OF THE
IMPERIALIST POLITICAL SYSTEM

. . . In the process of Japan's transition to imperialism, what kinds of changes did the power structure undergo in response to changes in the basic class relations? The answer, in brief, is that the absolute emperor system changed into a landowner-bourgeoisie emperor system. . . . The rapid development of capitalism after the Sino-Japanese war was accompanied by an increase in the social and economic power of the bourgeoisie and landowning classes, whose political influence now also expanded. This caused the political parties to exert stronger pressure on the bureaucratic Satsuma-Chōshū clique government, which consequently gave up its principles of "non-recognition of political parties" and "transcendentalism" [the principle that the government should be above politics] and sought a compromise with the parties. . . . Through Itō Hirobumi's repudiation of transcendental politics and participation in the organization of a political party [1900]

and through the Yamagata cabinet's proposal of new election and land tax laws [in 1900], the absolute bureaucracy won the support of landowners who controlled the rural communities and made common alliance with the urban bourgeoisie, thus hardening the system of exploiting the workers. This was the course toward imperialism which the governing classes consistently took during this period.

Let me explain. The founding of the Rikken Seiyūkai [Association for Constitutional Government] by Itō in 1900 should be viewed as a historic event in the restructuring of the political system from the top. This marked the first step in the establishment of a system of control by which a reactionary bloc composed of the absolute faction, the bourgeoisie, and the landlords would keep the workers and farmers under subjection. By uniting with the parties, the absolute faction moved to become a central force in developing Japanese imperialism. By incorporating the bourgeoisie into the political parties, the absolute faction further hoped to gain their support for the dominance of the bureaucracy in the imperialist political system of Japan. . . .

The bourgeoisie also steadily carried out its own imperialist program, using its alliance with the bureaucracy as a basis. For instance, when the House of Peers in the fifteenth Diet of 1900 opposed a bill asking for a tax increase of twenty million yen to finance military expenditures, the bourgeoisie, faced with the Boxer Rebellion and the prospect of an intensification in the struggle against czarist Russia, managed to push through passage of the bill. . . . The above indicates plainly that Japan had begun to advance rapidly along the road to imperialism and that its social system, as a whole, was entering upon the stage of imperialism, no matter how dependent, military, and feudal the character of that imperialism might seem. . . .

One factor which accounts for this reorganization in the power structure of the emperor system was the change in the basic class relations in Japan. As capitalism advanced, particularly after 1897, the number of wage workers increased and a labor movement gradually emerged. There was also the struggle of poor farmers and tenants. In the beginning, labor disputes were spontaneous, but the organization and solidarity of the workers advanced as their class consciousness deepened. . . . In the wake of rising class consciousness and early factory and rural labor organizations, the first socialist party in our country, the Social Democratic Party, was formed in May, 1901, to work for a social democratic revolution. The party was not yet able to rally the working masses, and its guiding principles were not yet purified as socialist thought. Nevertheless, the party's formation as an avant-garde organization to oppose the control of the bourgeois-landlord emperor system, which could continue in existence only by oppressing workers and farmers under slave-like conditions, was an important historical event. . . . The basic contradictions in the class relations in our country took on the palpable form of antagonism between the revolutionary bloc of the working class as the major force in an alliance with tenants and poor farmers and the reactionary bloc which was composed of the whole landlord class, privileged big bourgeoisie, and towering above all the emperor system. The alliance of the imperialist bourgeoisie and the landlord class was based upon their common political interests and directed against the rising working class in its struggle for socialism and a democratic revolution. In other words, the change in class relations more than anything else transformed and strengthened the emperor system.

CONCLUSION: THE NATURE AND MEANING OF THE RUSSO-JAPANESE WAR

Under the following two conditions Japan moved rapidly along the course toward an imperialist war whose aim was the redivision and monopoly of the China market: the establishment of a domestic system capable of oppression at home and aggression abroad, and on the international scene the acquisition of support and protection from an advanced imperialist power through the Anglo-Japanese Alliance. The demand that Korea and China be monopolized as dependable sources of raw materials and food and also as export markets for Japanese capitalism was so insistent, not only within the military circles and the bureaucracy but also within the bourgeoisie, that it became a policy acceptable to all of the ruling groups of the emperor's state. . . . The cabinet meeting of October 2, 1903, resolved to request "appropriations adequate to manage our enterprises in China and Korea" and concluded "it is an urgent necessity to expand our enterprises in China and Korea and to acquire rights and interests appropriate to the present status of our empire" so that Japan could cope with the commercial competition and overseas activities of the European powers and the United States. Therefore, we could characterize the Russo-Japanese war, I think, as an imperialist war which was caused by a combination of territorial ambition inherent in the emperor system and the demands of the imperialist bourgeoisie for markets. Moreover, it was a war which was guided by the bourgeoisie.

To sum up the historical problems in the establishment of Japanese imperialism, first, it seemed obvious at the turn of the century that Japan must transform itself rapidly into an imperialist nation in order to survive as an independent capitalist country within a world structure dominated by capitalism and imperialism. Accordingly, Japan took with vigor the course toward imperialism under the pressure of international conditions. Second, the imperialist redivision of China seemed an urgent necessity, particularly in view of Russian expansion on the continent. This was an outgrowth both of the traditional territorial and aggressive ambitions of the military and the bureaucracy under the emperor system and of the demands of the whole governing class, including the new bourgeoisie. Third, Japanese capitalism had no choice but to depend upon an enormous military establishment and rely upon advanced imperialist powers [rather than pursue an exclusively economic policy]. Fourth, Japan became an imperialist power by consolidating and strengthening the feudal parasitic landlord system, while also nurturing an imperialist bourgeoisie. In the process of Japan's rapid conversion to imperialism, the system of state control therefore underwent transformation . . . and the result was compromise, cooperation, and coalition among the absolute bureaucracy, the landowners, and the bourgeoisie.

Hilary Conroy

A REBUTTAL TO ECONOMIC DETERMINISM

Although much attention has been given to Japan's extraordinary economic growth in the past century, little detailed research has been done on the precise relationship between overseas activities and business enterprises in the period from the Sino-Japanese war to the 1930's. In the following selection, Hilary Conroy (1919–   ), Professor of Far Eastern History at the University of Pennsylvania and one of the foremost American scholars of Japanese imperialism and expansion, disputes in a pioneering effort the orthodox Marxist view of the underlying reasons for the annexation of Korea in 1910. He finds political and military motives to be more pertinent than economic ones. In fact, Japan's economic involvement in Korea came after rather than before annexation. Although he examines only the Korean issue, his findings suggest that economic determinism is a highly simplified way to explain the origins of modern Japanese empire, however important economic interests may become later. And it must be admitted that of all the explanations offered in this volume the economic one remains the most clouded by ignorance, confusion, and controversy.

ALONGSIDE the tendency in Western works to explain the annexation of Korea as a Japanese plot, there has developed in Japanese historical writing a tendency to explain it in the terminology of economic determinism, as the seemingly inevitable result of Japanese capitalism's reaching the "stage" of imperialism. One's first impulse might be to apply the label, Marxist, to this and dismiss it as a stereotype. However, consideration of the intellectual milieu out of which this interpretation emerged makes it clear that such an easy dismissal is unfair, for the argument has come, not merely out of Communist party line propaganda, but also out of dignified, scholarly, and sometimes heroic searching for explanations beyond the cheap jingoism that passed for scholarship in pre-World War II Japan.

. . . An example of this, with special reference to the Korean problem, is Hatada Takeshi's *Chōsen Shi* (History of Korea), published in 1951, which, although it covers the whole course of the Meiji period Japan-Korea relationship in a brief forty pages, gives considerable space to economic matters and makes some very strong statements in this regard. According to Hatada, as early as the 1880's Korea was becoming "bound in as a market for Japanese capitalism." Soon great quantities of Japanese textiles and other manufactures were being sent to Korea and "almost all" Korean foodstuff exports were being sent to Japan. "Japanese capitalism penetrated Korea and made it a market for its merchandise and a source of foodstuffs. Korea was an indispensable market for the growth of Japanese capitalism. . . . Thus the growth of Japanese capitalism had to retrieve political defeats and further promote economic penetration," which led into the Sino-Japanese War, etc. This is not to say that Hatada neglects all other factors to stress the economic. . . . [H]is words are sometimes suggestive of the Japanese government plot approach and he gives much space to diplomatic and political developments. But when he speaks of economic matters he uses the language

From Hilary Conroy, *The Japanese Seizure of Korea, 1868–1910* (Philadelphia: University of Pennsylvania Press, 1960), pp. 442–444, 484–491.

of economic determinism, capitalism "grows, binds in, penetrates," markets are "indispensable."

*   *   *

[However, for the period before 1900], the conclusion is clear and unequivocal: economic factors were negligible, insufficient, unimportant. The Sino-Japanese War, though it was Japan's first big step toward annexation of Korea, was not an economic war, caused neither by Sino-Japanese trade rivalry in Korea nor by the penetration of the peninsula by Japanese capitalism. This conclusion is suggested by the fact that during this period the economic stakes in Korea were small, involved only a few Japanese, and the Japanese government accepted ups and downs in regard to them with equanimity. Moreover, it is strongly reinforced by a most interesting recent trend among Japanese historians of the economic determinist persuasion. . . . [A]lthough the feudalism-capitalism-imperialism motif has remained central, greater knowledge of facts and reassessment of causes have led to an important modification of interpretation which has been generally accepted by all historians, even those noted for being most adamantly Marxist. This concerns specifically the problem of the Sino-Japanese War. It is now generally accepted that the causes of the Sino-Japanese War were *not* economic, to be found neither in the search for markets on the mainland of an expanding Japanese capitalism nor in economic-based class struggle in Japan. This is admitted even by Inoue Kiyoshi, the leading exponent of pure Marxist historicizing. Inoue, in his study of "The Formation of Japanese Imperialism," says specifically that the Sino-Japanese War did not grow out of Japanese capitalism. Rather "in actuality as well as on the surface" it was "planned, prepared for and carried out" by the "absolutist Emperor regime." It is interesting to observe in this connection that here we have the phenomenon of a Japanese Marxist coming very close to the plot theory which so many American writers

have favored. . . . At any rate, with support even from Inoue, we can confidently bury the economic hypothesis —for the period through the Sino-Japanese War.

However, thereafter, Inoue parts company with those Americans who presume that the plotting continued right on to World War II, and with any other sort of political or diplomatic explanation. Such, for him, is invalidated by the emergence of more automatic forces, namely capitalism and its offshoot, imperialism. After the Sino-Japanese War, says Inoue, Japanese capitalism, helped along by the war indemnity, moved into the industrial stage from which imperialism began. He asks the specific question, "when did Japanese imperialism begin?" and answers it by suggesting that the turning point was about 1900. It is "not important" he says whether one argues for 1900 or 1904–5 but "I [Inoue] consider 1900 as the turning point." In that year "Japan participated actively in an imperialist war [Peking expedition]" and inside the country with the appearance of Itō Hirobumi's Seiyūkai party the alliance between the bourgeoisie and the absolutist Emperor regime developed. Of course, this did not mean that the bourgeoisie had taken over political power, which happening did not occur until "the defeat in war [World War II]" but the Russo-Japanese War was "very different from the war of a decade before." The intervening development of industrial capitalism and the bourgeoisie made it truly a capitalist-imperialist war.

However, it should be noted that Inoue does not carry his argument beyond the Russo-Japanese War to the specifics of Korean annexation, which must certainly be considered the first territorial fruit of this developing imperialism. He does not show precisely how Japanese industrial capitalism and the bourgeoisie contributed to that annexation. And in fact, when he discusses Korea, which discussion is brief and limited to the period before the Russian war, the evidence he submits would seem to negate rather than support his hypothesis. He notes that at the time of the Sino-Japanese War Japan had insufficient money and power to carry out the reforms she contemplated in Korea, which implies that by the time of the Russo-Japanese War she had plenty of both. Yet he admits that to 1904 there was no significant Japanese investment, either public or private, in Korea. The only "productive capital investment" was the Seoul-Inchon railway which "was built more for military than for economic reasons." Hence, the idea that economic factors operating during the post-Sino-Japanese War period brought about the annexation of Korea, though implied by Inoue in his theoretical construction, is by no means proven by him. . . . [The] evidence is not conclusive as to pressure toward annexation generated by economic forces, but the slowness and weakness of the railroad and agriculture programs indicate clearly that there was no great impetus from Japanese capitalism in *them*. With regard to trade and its offshoot, banking, there is room for argument that in these areas the tentacles of Japanese capitalism were stretching forth without regard to political and diplomatic requirements or in such a way as to pull these along behind.

Here, . . . one could point to the pleadings of certain Japanese businessmen who thought there existed large economic opportunities in Korea. For example, Ōta Seizo, head of the Hakata (Kyushu) Chamber of Commerce, sent in proposals which the governor of Fukuoka transmitted to Foreign Minister Komura, under date of December 14, 1904. Japan, he argued, was "winning a complete victory" over Russia and it was time to plan postwar policy "so as to obtain a better place in the world market." Capital must be encouraged to move from "the inside [Japan]" to "the outside [Korea and Manchuria]." To do this, improvements were necessary "in a hurry." An "Oriental bank," improvement of the currency system, freeing of trade, mining, manufacturing, and "free going and coming" of Japanese to the mainland were necessary. The Japanese consul at Pusan, the chamber of commerce there, and the head of a Japanese

farmers' group of Kunsan were among others, who in 1904 addressed to the Foreign Office or the Ministry of Agriculture and Commerce similar urgings to pay heed to larger economic prospects in Korea.

Also K. Asakawa, whose contemporary study (1904) of the background of the Russo-Japanese War might be judged pro-Japanese, but certainly not Marxist, says in his introductory remarks that, "For Japan, the issues appear to be only partly political, but mainly economical. . . . Among the most remarkable tendencies of Japan's economic life of recent years has been the enormous growth of her population, along with an immense growth of her trade and industries." He puts the number of Japanese in Korea at "nearly 30,000" and, quoting Finance Ministry figures, he shows the total foreign trade of Japan to have grown from 49,742,831 yen in 1873 to 606,637,959 yen in 1903, of which the Korean trade amounted to 20,676,000 yen in 1903. This last figure represented an increase of some six and one-half million yen over the Japan-Korea trade total for 1897. Asakawa is at pains to emphasize the importance of this trade and also the importance of Japanese immigration to Korean agriculture in building a foundation for his argument that "community of interest" demanded that Japan assume an active role of "assistance" to Korean "sovereignty." But he does not consider negative aspects of this, such as the fact that few of the Japanese immigrants took up agriculture in Korea and almost none thought in terms of a long stay, or the value of the trade compared with the cost of protecting it. And again with Asakawa, as with the other contemporary accounts which stress economic themes, there is a strong tendency to emphasize the future. The future would presumably bring the realization of economic prospects hitherto only dimly seen.

However, the future, to annexation at least, remained dim. Figures for five years of Japanese "protection" (1905–9) show three years of rapid increase, but then sharp decline. Annexation (1910) can hardly be called the outgrowth of an expanding trade. Rather it seems to have rescued the trade from decline. . . .

Certainly Japanese businessmen were disappointed with the course of affairs. Mr. Ōta of the Hakata Chamber of Commerce appealed again to the Foreign Ministry in 1906, arguing that "Government regulations" and "poor equipment" were preventing the realization of economic opportunities in Korea and also Manchuria. But by 1910, even with annexation, the businessmen could not refrain from expressing dissatisfaction. *Tōkyō Keizai Zasshi* [Tokyo Economic Journal] "on reading the explanation of Korean annexation" had the following complaint: "We agree with the political aspects but we are disappointed in the economic. For ten years, says the Government, the rate of tariff between Japan and Korea will be preserved. Thus exports and imports must pay duty. . . . This is not good. Foreign Minister Komura gives as the main reason for annexation political necessity, and he says we must not affect the interests of foreign powers adversely in Korea. . . . We oppose. We say remove the tariff and do not worry about the interests of other foreigners."

This evidence may not be sufficient to defeat the thesis that Japanese capitalism, accelerating rapidly after 1900, was the motive force behind the Korean annexation, but it would seem to throw it into serious question. And on the level of scholarly interpretation one further piece of evidence remains to be introduced. A very recent development in Japanese scholarship seems to indicate that even among those of Marxist inclination doubts of the importance of the economic factor *post*-1900 also are beginning to appear. This is clearly indicated in a "review and criticism" of writings on "the formation of Japanese imperialism" by Furuya Tetsuo, which appeared in December, 1956. Furuya is anxious to support the thesis that the Russo-Japanese War was an imperialist war from the Japanese side, the outgrowth of an imperialism that had its beginnings in Japanese participation among European powers in the Boxer affair—"the first imperialist step for Ja-

pan." But he is troubled at the lack of economic factors in it. He finds that two (non-Marxist) Japanese historians, Shimomura Fujio and Fujimura Michio, have gone so far as to say that "the Russo-Japanese war was not done by the Japanese bourgeoisie nor did it originate in the demands of the bourgeoisie toward the Manchurian market." However, Furuya argues, these gentlemen "have made a mistake. Their definition of imperialism is not correct." He agrees that the Russo-Japanese War was not the result of the Japanese bourgeois' seeking mainland markets, but "whether a war is imperialist or not does not depend entirely on the internal economic development of capitalism." Rather "in a later developing country" such as Japan "the international political situation may exert more influence on decision making than the internal economic structure." Thus, he concludes that the formation of Japanese imperialism and its external advance *can* be seen in the period between the Boxer Rebellion and the Russo-Japanese War.

Since we are concerned here with the assessment of economic matters in their relation to the Korean annexation, we need not argue whether non-economic imperialism is in fact imperialism. . . . But Furuya's sense of the need to eliminate the economic factor, even as he defends the idea that Japan was propelled into Korea and Manchuria by imperialist urges developing around 1900, would seem to be highly significant, indeed, in pointing to the probability that economic reasons for the Russo-Japanese War, and hence for the Korean annexation, were nonexistent or very minor. Certainly he would have pointed them out if he could have found them, for with them he could have demolished the arguments of Shimomura and Fujimura and supported his own imperialism argument much more effectively. As it is, we must come to the conclusion that even those scholars who are most anxious to follow the projection of [pre-World War II] Rōnō [Labor-Farmer] and Kōza [Lectures (on capitalism)] scholarship into a capitalism-imperialism explanation of the development of Japanese expansion on the Asian mainland are unable to do so, not only for the pre-Sino-Japanese War period but also for the Russo-Japanese War period.

We therefore arrive at our conclusion . . . Economic matters had no important effect in determining the Japanese course toward annexation of Korea.

V. PREMEDITATED MURDER
OR ACCIDENTAL DEATH?

George Kerr

BLUEPRINT FOR CONQUEST

A strong undercurrent in several of the previous selections is the assumption that Japan's rapid acquisition of empire was no mere accident. Some writers are content to emphasize built-in militarism and deep-seated ambitions; but others go beyond this to allege the existence of a long-range government plot dating back to 1868, if not earlier, to seize surrounding territory in East Asia. Japan went systematically from success to success. Displays of caution and hesitation were simply temporary tactics geared to an unchanging strategy of domination. Japan is made to appear ruthless, calculating, and power-mad. Japan "thirsted" or Japan "craved" is representative of some of the wording. Mention was made in the introduction of the wide-spread belief in the 1930's in the existence of the Tanaka Memorial, Japan's plan for world conquest. George Kerr (1911–   ), author of works on Okinawa and Formosa, wrote the following article during his military service in World War II. In it he argues that a blueprint, the Kodama Report of 1902, predated the Tanaka Memorial. The document is deemed authentic by virtue of Japan's subsequent behavior, and its proposals are seen as forming an important link in the schemes which culminated in the Greater East Asia Co-Prosperity Sphere. The supposition that Japan deliberately planned for empire lingers on today in articles, textbooks, and doctoral dissertations.

A BLUEPRINT for Japan's conquest of southeast Asia, the Philippines, and the Indies was brought to the attention of the world forty years ago. It was complete to detailed logistic tables calculating the time required to move five divisions suddenly into Indo-China, there to prepare for attack on Malaya, the Netherlands colonies, and American possessions in exactly the sequence ultimately followed in 1941–42. It contained explicit plans for the development of Formosa as a great base for southward expansion, a base necessary for the preparation of striking power close to the objects of attack and vital to the security of Japan's overseas communication. It suggested advantageous centers for organization and some methods of espionage, and the use of diplomacy and diplomatic agents. This plan, the *Kodama Report,*[1] its exposure, and the subsequent indifference shown by democratic governments, although its recommendations were carried out step by step before their eyes, bear review now as we discuss international checks upon aggression.

In the 1930's the Japanese announced and developed the program for a "Greater East Asia Co-Prosperity

[1] No copy of this document nor of the issues of *Echo de Paris* which exposed it are known to exist in the archives or libraries of the United States. Photostatic copies of these issues were obtained from the Paris files.

From George Kerr, "Kodama Report: Plan for Conquest," *Far Eastern Survey*, XIV, no. 14 (July 18, 1945), 185–190.

Sphere," and the world thereby was warned that the Japanese Government believed itself ready and able to embark upon hemispheric conquest. The economic phases of it were well advanced on the Continent and the time seemed ripe (because of the successive crises in Europe and the outspoken isolationism in America) to press on with the more obvious military aspects of imperial dominion. In the late 1920's the *Tanaka Memorial* had been published, a document allegedly addressed in July of 1927 to the Emperor, setting forth in outline the most grandiose schemes of world conquest. A flurry of press comment and a ripple of diplomatic embarrassment followed the exposure, but little more. In the preceding decade, also at a time when the European powers were involved in war and America was struggling to remain neutral, the Japanese Government presented the Chinese Government with the infamous *Twenty-one Demands,* which if accepted would have destroyed China's vestiges of sovereignty and independence. The world should have been warned then—but it was not —of the very real and persistent character of official Japanese plans for the conquest of the Asiatic mainland. One could go back through one hundred and fifty years noting Japanese programs for conquest, some set forth by private individuals and some proposed by responsible members of Government. One most exact in detail and most precise in fulfillment was the so-called *Kodama Report* of 1902, published as a sensational exposure in the Paris press in 1905 during the Russo-Japanese War.

General Baron Kodama Gentaro was Governor-General of Formosa from 1898 to 1906. He was a man of great importance in both civil and military administration at Tokyo and exercised the powers of a viceroy in the new colony of Formosa. His appointment to the governorship of this raw and troublesome outpost was looked upon as political exile by his partisans, but as the contents of this report and subsequent events have demonstrated, he was sent there to expedite Japan's plans for developing Formosa into a primary base for aggression throughout southeast Asia.

From out of Japan's feudal days and the struggle for power at the time of the Restoration there had developed a rivalry between two schools of aggressive thought: the one, predominantly the Army school, advocated expansion to the north and west, over the Korean peninsula and westward on the Continent, principally at the expense of China and Russia; the other, identified more or less with Navy ambitions, advocated expansion to the south, overseas, involving seizure of Chinese coastal territory and all European colonies in southeast Asia. Some evidences of that division remain today in Japanese councils and in prosecution of the war. The ultimate objectives have remained the same in all cases, namely, the conquest of the entire Far East by imperial Japan. It becomes evident from the *Kodama Report* that the author, an Army man sent southward to Formosa, must have exerted great influence in coordinating the two drives.

CONQUEST OF FORMOSA COSTLY

Formosa was hard to take, and the first seven years (after 1895) were enormously costly to the Tokyo government. The Army party, making ready for war with Russia, was jealous of every yen and of every unit diverted southward. Criticism was sharp at Tokyo and pressure was great; some of the most shortsighted Army partisans even proposed that Japan sell the as yet unprofitable island so that undivided attention could be given to the conquest of Manchuria and the Continent beyond. General Baron Kodama, however, appears to have proposed a course of action which would supplement the Continental policy and in due time secure for Japan, at a minimum cost, not only the China coast, but a vast empire among the ex-European colonies in the south. His program was delayed by the First World War and by subsequent economic disasters, but events of 1937–42 followed the geographic course and sequence which he set forth.

On January 10, 11, and 12, in 1905, the Paris newspaper, *Echo de Paris,* published what purported to be a secret document prepared by Kodama and submitted to the Cabinet at Tokyo in 1902. The Japanese Minister at Paris instantly denounced it as spurious but, however the French came by the text, one is almost forced to accept its authenticity through *ex post facto* evidence. It is noteworthy that throughout the document Baron Kodama referred to the regions of southeast Asia as "our future possessions." It was not a case of "if we conquer" but "when we have conquered."

PRINCIPAL PARTS OF REPORT

The report contains five principal parts:

1. a response to criticism directed against the administration of the Governor-General in Formosa;
2. a statement of reasons why Japanese action should be directed toward the Continent (Manchuria) at that moment;
3. an exposition of the impossibility of carrying out a successful attack upon French Indo-China at that time (1902);
4. the detailed reasons for delaying such an attack, and how ultimately it should be accomplished; and
5. the plans for mobilizing isolated Formosa to play a pre-eminent part in the drive along the China coast, into Indo-China, and thence into all European colonial possessions and into the Philippines.

Addressing himself to the expansionists who advocated an immediate move southwards, Kodama had this to say:

To the eager eyes of partisans of a Japanese drive toward the south rather than toward the north, in order to provide, they say, an outlet for the excess population of Honshu, Formosa is no more than a simple bridge, ready as an aid to an immediate leap toward Fukien, Canton, the Kwangs [Kwangtung, Kwangsi Provinces], and Indo-China. . . .
We have been in Formosa scarcely six years.
For a long time our occupation was limited to the cities on the littoral. It has been only two years since our penetration of the in-

terior has been going forward. And our commerce is still very small, a time when the population is far from being rallied to us, and when we are only beginning to know a portion of the richness of the island. This [then] is the moment chosen by our press to bring forth the most marvelous projects, to declare that the "Japanese" island of Formosa *ought to be,* that is *is capable of becoming,* and that *it is even now* a completely prepared stage on the way to conquest of the South.
Can it be then that it is our six local [Formosan] battalions, or even our three mixed brigades (scarcely enough to garrison a territory equal to a tenth of the area of Japan) who are going to begin a victorious march upon Hong Kong, Canton, Hanoi, Saigon, Manila, Bangkok and Batavia? They cannot be serious. We are not uncontested sovereigns of the China Sea as we are of our Inland Sea. These infatuated expansionists forget that even if we had, by dint of effort, the best and most numeorus army of the Far East we do not have the navy indispensable for convoying this army 2,000 miles from our islands, to protect it, and to supply it with munitions and matériel. . . .

SELECTION OF ADVERSARY

The consequence of this situation is very simple: Should we seek an adversary in combat, we ought to enquire which adversary disturbs us most by his expansion and whose naval forces can injure us the least.
At present, in my opinion, the enemy most immediately threatening [us], and the most vulnerable too, is at the north. The actual insufficiency of naval and military forces in Indo-China, and the insignificant position of the French merchant marine, which would only with difficulty permit of large troop convoys, give weight, it is true, in favor of an immediate attack upon the Asiatic possessions of France. But in the hypothesis of a victory what would we gain? A colony producing rice, [a colony] whose sub-soil is rich in minerals but which has not yet established either railroads or sufficiently useful ports, except for Saigon [which is] 2,000 miles from Nagasaki.

. . . Further, General Kodama explains that a war with France at the moment of writing (1902) would be premature. Not that he would renounce for that reason a conquest of Indo-China, but in his opinion conquest of French possessions in Asia could not be carried out with success until towards 1908 or 1910. . . .

LOGISTICS OF ATTACK

In arguing that an attack southward in 1902 would be premature, Kodama went to great lengths to present a technical analysis of logistics, using comparative tables showing the troop movements which could be effected in 1902 and in 1910. The time consumed in moving five divisions would be almost the same, but in the meantime the Japanese would have developed Formosa to enormous advantage as a naval base and advanced military depot. The French meanwhile would have developed the railroads and ports of French Indo-China so that, once invaded, internal movement would be greatly facilitated. And China would have ceded Kwangchow to the Japanese, to be used by them as a port of entry for an overland march to the borders of Tonkin, while a frontal attack would be possible by sea. . . .

This problem [of secure communications], today insoluble, will no longer exist for us and the most satisfactory possible solution will have been achieved if, in the meantime, the island of Formosa will have been prepared to play the preponderant role I have conceived for it and [here] reveal at length. I beg of Your Excellency the greatest attention possible in the examination of the projects which follow:

Bring the metropolitan government appropriation up to 10,000,000 yen for administrative expenses of the island *in such a way as to Japanize all primary education*.

Bring the annual military appropriation up to 15,000,000 yen in order to double the number of local battalions, to construct new barracks, to complete the hydrographic surveys of the coasts of the islands and of Fukien, and to maintain a naval station at Makung [Mako or Bako] in the Pescadores.

Establish a sanitorium [rehabilitation center] and an isolated camp, with arsenal and foundry, not far from the slopes of Mt. Niitaka.

The quantity of arms, munitions and provisions to be established is approximately as follows:

> 30 depot batteries
> 660,000 shrapnel shells
> 100,000 rifles

> 100,000,000 cartridges
> 3,600,000 bushels of rice
> 3,000,000 bushels of wheat

Finish the construction of the railway from Keelung to Takao and double the line. Dredge and fortify the ports of Keelung, Tamsui, Makung, Anping and Takao. Strengthen the communications between the ports of Tamsui and Keelung by a canal, using the waters of the Tamsui River. Secure the construction of a Japanese railway linking Foochow with the Hankow-Canton line.

Create Japanese consulates and intelligence agencies at Foochow, Macao, Canton, Pakhoi, Along, Hanoi, Tourane, and Saigon.

After the realization of these several projects, all of which do not have the same urgency, but all of which, taken together, do not seem to me to require an expenditure above 120,000,000 yen, divisible over eight years, I estimate that everything will then be prepared to render victorious at a minimum cost the conquest of all foreign territories in the South, through the appropriate organization of [the potential of] Formosa.

REACTIONS TO PUBLICATION

The publication of the *Kodama Report* called forth immediate official repudiation. Motono Ichiro, then Japanese Minister at Paris, issued statements to the press in which he took note of various discrepancies in the text, such as the dating, and certain phraseology which he alleged could not have been used by Kodama. In the absence of the Japanese text it is impossible to verify his arguments, but the well-known ambiguities of Japanese chronology weaken his refutation, for there often can be a discrepancy of as much as three years through the use of "reign-dates," and it is upon these that Montono's primary objections were based. The dating of the alleged *Report* at Keelung rather than at Taihoku might be explained by the fact that the Keelung Fortress Headquarters were then the principal military offices on the island, and quite logically could have been used by Kodama as Commander-in-Chief of Taiwan forces. These are minor points, overshadowed by the cumulative evidence of later years: the consistent fulfillment of the program, step by step.

The Paris press generally took note

of the sensational exposure made by the *Echo de Paris*. The *Journal des Débats* reprinted most of it, with the Japanese denial and with comment as well on the dangerous implications for all countries of an article then current in the Japanese *Diplomatic Review*, which proposed Japanese hegemony for all of Asia. . . .

AMERICAN MILITARY UNIMPRESSED

. . . The document appears to have aroused interest in American military circles only so far as it presented a nicely stated problem in logistics in a remote part of the world.

Nevertheless, Kodama's school of military thought prevailed. Russia was attacked first and temporarily removed as a threat through the victory off Tsushima and the Treaty of Portsmouth. Japan's economy was so weakened at home, however, and the resistance of the Formosan-Chinese themselves on the island so costly and prolonged that development of Formosa went forward much more slowly than Kodama had anticipated. By 1910 the European war was in the offing and opportunities for further Continental operations presented themselves with the breakup of the Manchu Empire and subsequent disorder in China.

LESSONS TO BE LEARNED

The specific lesson to be learned needs little discussion: Japanese policy since 1868 has shown a singular consistency and uniformity, an undeviating purposefulness, that has been objective, cold, and calculating to a degree unconceivable in American thinking. No true democracy could project such grandiose schemes for aggression; no democratic government could so commit future generations to conquest and inevitable conflict with other peoples and have its responsible leaders connive in the planning. . . . The Japanese are enormously sensitive to a tradition of divine destiny, projected from a history which, though highly fictionalized, is nevertheless very real to the individual Japanese. An acute sense of the past, distorted and fed on fiction, stimulates people to think also in terms of the long-distant future. . . . Japan's sense of national unity and destiny permits the ruling class to plan not for decades but for centuries, and in cold blood to commit unborn generations to inevitable conflict.

Hilary Conroy

UNEXPECTED HAPPENINGS

Professor Conroy makes a second appearance; this time to comment on the emotionally charged subject of Japan's annexation of Korea in 1910. Japan's excesses there as a colonial master are still remembered with anger and bitterness. Conroy began his research with the expectation of discovering documents which would support the plot thesis but instead found that Japanese statesmen and diplomats, on the whole, were not eager to seize opportunities for expansion. They were cautious, restrained, and negotiated in good faith—realists whose chief concern was how best to protect Japan's national interests. To allege a long-range plot is like saying the United States schemed from 1789 to 1898 to annex Hawaii and the Philippines. Within the Meiji government there was improvisation, not calculation. Rational bureaucrats and not conspirators or continentalists made policy. And it should further be remembered that many of Japan's contemporaries around the world thought it was doing the work of civilization in Korea. In Conroy's analysis, Japan fell victim to unexpected events and unquestioning reliance on the doctrines of power politics, showing in the process the inadequacy of realism untempered by idealism. This puts Japan's international morality, until 1910 at least, on a par with all the other powers—hardly better or worse.

IT might be argued by some that there is no point in trying to establish what the Japanese government "aimed" to do with regard to Korea. It is what they *did* that counts, and further what they did may be taken as the best indication of what they aimed to do. But premeditated murder and accidental death are very different things in courts of law, though the difference may be academic to the dead man. And it would seem to be of some consequence in working toward an understanding of the motive forces in international relations, as well as toward a fair appraisal of the Meiji government, to know whether they schemed the seizure of Korea, or were pushed into it by forces beyond their control, or fell into it through lack of foresight; whether honorable intentions turned dishonorable through ineptness, or whether they were dishonorable to begin with. And by what standard do we measure them?

For a standard of measurement we might take American Far Eastern policy, which, while considered by some . . . to have been inept, is not generally adjudged to have been villainous, even though it included two annexations (Hawaii and the Philippines). Indeed, Theodore Roosevelt seems to have been quite willing to equate this American interest in the Philippines with the Japanese interest in Korea, at least to trade diplomatically on that basis. How far is such a comparison justified? Or to ask it another way, how far was the Japanese "opening" of Korea like the American "opening" of Japan? Completely different—for the Japanese "aimed" to take Korea and the United States had no such aim as regards Japan. However, a skillful anti-Americanist might build a great plot theory from Perry to MacArthur to show that the ultimate American aim all along was control of Japan. Such a theory might be facile, though it would be false. And yet, the very possibility of

From Hilary Conroy, *The Japanese Seizure of Korea: 1868–1910* (Philadelphia: University of Pennsylvania Press, 1960), pp. 82–83, 181, 185–86, 219–223, 254–57, 325, 331–32, 379–81, 440–41, 492.

contriving such a theory should make us careful of an easy acceptance of a plot theory in the Japan-Korea case, even though we dislike what the Japanese did to Korea.

*   *   *

. . . [T]he image of the Japanese as a two-faced people and of Japanese foreign policy as being continuously devious from the Meiji era to Pearl Harbor is a very strong one in the Western world. Of course, no thoughtful person puts this in absolute terms, but the image is damaging enough that it would seem desirable that those who study the Japanese record in international affairs try to estimate whether they find deviousness and dishonesty sufficiently worse than the norm of international conduct to warrant special comment; or if they do not find the Japanese record especially odious in this regard, to try to explain why such an image has developed. The present study, limited as it is to the Meiji era and the Korean episode, cannot provide a conclusive answer, but, since the record of the process of Japanese assumption of control over Korea has given a strong impetus to the development of the image, a close look at that process should contribute to our understanding of how far the image is true, how far distorted.

*   *   *

We are aware, of course, that Japan did fight China in 1894 and oust Chinese influence from Korea, and that this . . . could be taken as evidence presumptive that the Japanese government was planning the coup de grâce many years before. But unfortunately for the theory, though perhaps fortunately for our faith in the human race (to 1893), it is not supported by evidence *minutus;* the pattern of Japanese activity in Korea . . . is much too inconsistent and, yes, blundering to be part of an evil plan.

*   *   *

. . . [I]t is clear that Japanese policy makers needed no great plot to bring them around to a re-evaluation of Korea policy in 1893. The following considera-

tions posed it: (1) Caution and conciliation had resulted in Chinese ascendancy and chaotic political conditions in Korea; there was no sign that either was abating. (2) Greatly augmented Russian power in the Far East was forecast for the near future. (3) Political parties were making a desperate bid to break the power of the oligarchy in Japan; in this struggle they were joining reactionary groups to make stronger foreign policy into a popular demand, one which Japanese friends of Korea, Japanese residents in Korea, nearly everyone interested in Korea supported. Thus, past experience, future prognosis, and present pressures seemed to demand a bold move in, around, or for Korea. Yet the oligarchs hesitated. What was the realistic thing to do? No decision was made in 1893, but 1894 brought what Foreign Minister Mutsu called "various unexpected happenings."

*   *   *

Japanese policy makers came into the year 1894 in a mood of dissatisfaction with the drift of affairs in Korea and on the defensive in the face of demands from the Diet for a bolder foreign policy. Within the inner group of the oligarchy itself there was division of opinion, with Yamagata and military men generally exerting a pressure for greater audacity, while Itō [prime minister for the second time] and his foreign minister, Mutsu, held the line for caution. Between Itō and Mutsu there was some slight disagreement. This has been described by Shinobu Seizaburō, author of the standard study of Mutsu's diplomacy in this period, in the following way. "Both Itō and Mutsu agreed on the basic objective of peace . . . but there was a minor difference. Itō's idea was 'insofar as possible without breaking the peace, we shall maintain the nation's honor.' Mutsu said, 'Within the limitation of not impairing the nation's honor, we shall to the utmost seek peaceful means to settle the situation.' " In other words Mutsu in the hour of crisis would be less adamant as a holdout for caution than Itō. But, as Shinobu also points out, Mutsu felt himself to be on the horns of a diplomatic dilemma, wherein the successful negotiation of treaty revision precluded "positive action" in Korea, yet a solution to the Korean problem was "absolutely necessary."

Mutsu's first attention in 1894 was to treaty revision. He undertook negotiations directly and exclusively with Great Britain, which had long stood as the principal obstacle to the progress of Japanese aspirations for treaty equality. These negotiations promised to be of the most delicate sort, with the British, fully aware that they were doing Japan a great favor, ready to delay the proceedings at the slightest provocation. Thus Mutsu had to spend most of the month of February reassuring the British government that Japan had in mind no such drastic measures as unilateral denunciation of the treaties. . . . The late spring and early summer of 1894 were the critical months for these negotiations, and it is difficult to conceive of the Japanese government as deliberately fomenting a Korean crisis at this time. However, two spectacular events, the murder of Kim Ok-kiun[1] in Shanghai on March 28 and the dispatch of Chinese troops to Korea to suppress the Tonghak rebellion on June 6, brought on a crisis situation as a result of which Japan embarked on war with China and a single-minded effort to force "reform" in Korea. Such drastic actions would seem to imply bold and willful contrivance; but when one watches the process of policy decision unfold step by step one is struck by the extent to which improvisation rather than calculation underlay the moves of Japanese policy makers. Hesitant, nervous, flustered, and, ultimately, frustrated are adjectives which might be applied to the oligarchs as they tried to solve the Korean problem by bold, swift action in 1894–95. Foreign Minister Mutsu in a memorandum to Itō, dated August 16, 1894, urging the cabinet to decide on a "fundamental policy toward Korea," used words

which ring back again and again as one observes the trend of Japanese policy through these years and beyond—toward the eventual conclusion that only by annexation could the Korean problem be solved. He said: "The Korean situation as anticipated and prepared for at the time Ōtori [Keisuke, minister to Seoul, 1893–94] was sent to Korea developed and changed unexpectedly; various unexpected happenings have led step by step into the present situation."

* * *

. . . At this point a conclusion may be drawn as to when the Japanese made the decision to oust Chinese influence from Korea by force. It was not in 1876 or 1882 or 1884 or 1885 or 1893 or even in the spring of 1894 at the time of the murder of Kim and the Tonghak risings. It was taken only two weeks before the sinking of the *Kowshing* [a Chinese troopship] (July 25, 1894), which event marked the opening of hostilities. Of course, a climate conducive to this decision was produced by a number of background factors, the success of China in asserting the dependent state relationship since 1885, the pressure for intervention by anti-government groups in Japan, increasing military preparedness and confidence in military circles in Japan, awareness of a developing security problem versus Russia, as well as the more immediate causes of tension (the Kim and Tonghak affairs). However, caution died hard in the oligarchs, especially Itō, and, even as they arrived at the conclusion that realism now called for bold action, Itō sent Ōtori a special direct wire urging him not to be rash.

The Sino-Japanese war was for Japan a short, glorious, and popular war. At its declaration all segments of the Japanese political scene immediately closed ranks behind the oligarchs to support the war effort. People's rights advocates were especially enthusiastic, for they saw it as a war for progress and civilization. . . . When the Seventh Diet convened in October, all the fiery opposition to the cabinet which had characterized the earlier diets had disappeared. In four days it passed all government measures pre-

---

[1] Kim was a Korean reformer who had gone into exile after an unsuccessful attempt to take over the Korean government in 1884. He had many sympathizers in Japan, mainly among the critics of Meiji foreign policy. [Editor's note.]

sented to it, voted a huge war appropriation, and adjourned.

Thus, from the viewpoint of the oligarchs, the move into war was politically
astute, for it tamed the opposition parties. Also, it became quickly a military
success, with Japanese forces piling up
victories on land and sea. With this the
case, and since we have observed that
the viewpoint of the oligarchy after the
affair of 1873 was that of realism par
excellence in politics and diplomacy, the
question that needs to be asked is perhaps not so much why did Itō and fellow
policy makers undertake the war as why
the degree of hesitation and trepidation
which their records reveal. There is every evidence that their idea of war was
that which "realists" in nation state diplomacy have generally accepted, that it
is an unfortunate, but sometimes necessary, extension of diplomacy. If any of
them felt moral or religious compunc-
tions about it, they did not allow these
feelings to enter their policy delibera-
tions. However, they did have a "fear" of
war, . . . a concern lest its limited realistic objectives become obscured in emotion and anger, with people at large, or
"public opinion," becoming involved in
unreal emotional issues, delusions, and
impractical idealism. Theirs was a fear
of those uncontrollable factors which a
war situation might unleash. All this
would seem to qualify them as realists
in [George] Kennan's best sense of the
word—sober professionals in foreign policy, working in the interest of (Japanese) national security. They were as
wary as they could be, given the exigen-
cies, of merely short-term opportunism,
and for this reason it is not sufficient to
say that they decided for war in order to
quiet the political opposition in Japan,
or to give Japan's military machine a
chance to show its muscles, or to make a
territorial grab. These were background
considerations, temptations to war, but
they were secondary. The main point
was the Korean problem, as, in the eyes
of the oligarchs, it related to Japanese
security. And though they became convinced that China must be ousted from
the affairs of the peninsula before a solu-

tion to that problem satisfactory to Japan
could be found, they were aware that this
alone would not necessarily assure a
"good outcome." The post-China era
might bring other complications in Korea, particularly in the area of relations
with Western powers. Hence the hesitation. Hence also the care to go to war in
"Christian style," with Red Cross units
and lawyers versed in international law
accompanying the military forces, and
to avoid affronts to Westerners in Korea.

*   *   *

Although 1896 saw Japan's Korea policy again in disarray and her policy makers in gloom at the prospect of an indefi-
nite prolongation and intensification of
the sense of insecurity about Korea, "a
dagger pointed at the home islands," the
next decade was kind to Japan. By the
end of 1905 a series of fortuitous events
and a mighty Japanese military effort
had eliminated Russia from Korean affairs and even given Japan control of
the south Manchurian area, which constituted precisely the double guarantee
of freedom of action in the peninsular
kingdom which her policy makers had
wanted in 1895. In addition, other powers with interests there, especially Britain and the United States, had sworn off
"meddling" in Korea, being content to
leave it to Japan to do the "world's work"
of remedying her condition as a "derelict
state" and confer on her the "benefits of
modern civilization."

*   *   *

. . . In our modern world "good" governments do not apologize for pursuing
national security. In fact a citizen living
under a "good" government is not considered a "good" citizen unless he has
some concern in this regard, and certainly a public official must have great
concern. Otherwise he becomes a "security risk." Of course, it is recognized that
the position of a "good" citizen under a
"bad" government is anomalous, for a
"bad" government will deliberately go
beyond the legitimate pursuit of national

security into the illegitimate pursuit of aggression. However, inasmuch as both of these pursuits take a nation outside its own borders and involve it in efforts to influence other states, the boundary between them is difficult to ascertain in terms of extent of interference alone. This difficulty is heightened by the natural tendency of any given nation to set its own security requirements higher than another nation would consider necessary.

In the case of Japan versus Korea, it could be argued that, since the powers came around to approving Japan's interference there during the Russo-Japanese War, such would constitute a sufficient admission that the Korean problem was legitimately a security problem for Japan. But this neglects the possibility that aggression was being acquiesced to for reasons of impotence or disinterest. Hence the question of means becomes important as a yardstick for measuring the guilt of Japan, for ascertaining whether her actions in Korea could be classified as those of a "good" government pursuing legitimate security interests or those of a "bad" government bent on aggression. The outcome, annexation in 1910, of course, immediately suggests the latter, aggression. But lest our judgment be too hasty, we should recall that though the United States annexed both Hawaii and the Philippines in 1898, we would be reluctant to call these simply instances of aggression. And, in fact, when we examine the documents which reveal the thinking of those leaders of the Japanese government who organized the Korean program 1905 to 1910, we find that, even though free of interference by other nations, they *were* anxious to be benevolent, to develop the Japanese-Korean relationship in ways that would be acceptable and helpful to Koreans while meeting their own security requirements. Thus within that restricted framework which required that Japanese must come first they may be called doctors of civilization, seeking to bring enlightenment and reform to Korea, not with idealistic balderdash but with realism of the best enlightenment-

self-interest variety. At least, they seem to have begun that way.

*   *   *

. . . What was Itō's plan [when he became Resident-General of Korea in 1904]? It was *not* annexation and not brutal tyranny. It was to establish a sort of triangular balance, Residency General, Korean court, and Korean reform ministry, through which Japanese-Korean co-operation could obtain to produce reform and modernization of Korea and which would render Japan secure from any possible threat launched via Korea. Of the two objectives, the second, Japanese security, was the overriding one, but Itō was confident that both could be obtained, and within the limits set by security he strove hard for co-operation. . . .

However, by July, 1909, we can say with confidence that the collective opinion of the Japanese oligarchy was that Itō's system was not enough to meet the requirements of Japanese security. . . . Things had not worked out well. The Korean court had caused trouble, the disbanded army had caused trouble, there seemed to be no end of riots and unrest. More Japanese power in Korea was an obvious remedy. Itō himself was disappointed and there is little doubt that, whether he sought a longer trial period for his system or not, before his death he gave acquiescence to the proposition that if things did not improve annexation would be "necessary." Itō's assassination [October, 1909] took the heart out of those who wished to try restraint a little longer and, though Sone [Arasuke, his successor as Resident General] made an effort to hold out, he broke literally and physically as the annexation band wagon began to roll.

In July, 1910, General Terauchi [Masatake, Minister of War for several years before his appointment as first Governor General of Korea] settled in Seoul and "it was as though a chill had passed over the city. He said little in public but . . . things began to happen. Four newspapers were suspended in a night. An item in their columns was objectionable. Let others be careful . . . every day brought its tale of arrests," as "the hardest and most relentless form of Imperial administration" was fastened on Korea.

So once again Japan's realistic diplomacy left the high road of enlightened self-interest and went down the low road of suppression, brutality, and murder.

*   *   *

This movement of realism toward reaction is a most interesting phenomenon. Speaking in the specific terms of the Korean issue, we would ask why, in the last analysis, was it Terauchi and not Itō? Was not Itō's brand of realism sufficient for Japan's security interests? Certainly it would seem so to an outsider. Is the pull from Itō to Terauchi, then, to be explained simply as the result of the machinations of the reverse idealists, Uchida and company [Uchida Ryōhei, head of the Black Dragon Society and protégé of Toyama Mitsuru]. The story of their activities . . . indicates clearly enough that they exerted themselves to undo Itō's efforts to practice enlightened realism. But do they deserve the full credit, which they so boastfully claim, for this. One suspects not. They could plot and scheme, persuade and threaten, but they were after all only on the fringes not in the seats of government power. And Japan's Meiji oligarchs, who did occupy those seats, were by no means inept at thwarting opposition groups, even those which were well organized and had much popular backing. On the Korean issue, they were utterly impervious to the arguments of their socialist critics, . . . yet even Itō could not bring himself to squelch Uchida and company, not even when he knew that they were undermining his own position. Why? The evidence discussed above does not, we think, admit the easy answer of hypocrisy on the part of Itō and others. Rather, it would seem, a more complex phenomenon was at work. This

may be stated in general terms as "the susceptibility of Realism to Reaction in international affairs." Here, we would suggest, lies the key to the waning of liberalism and the waxing of reaction in a climate of realist diplomacy. And here is the rock on which Kennan and [Hans] Morganthau and [Reinhold] Niebuhr and all the other advocates of cold and careful realism in international politics founder. They expect Itō and enlightened realism, but it is Terauchi's stage they set.

This may seem too large a conclusion to be drawn from our single Japan-Korea case, but there are good reasons for thinking it is not. These revolve around the proposition that the basic force at work in Japan's descent from enlightened realism to brutality in the treatment of Korea is the keystone in the arch of all realistic diplomacy, national security.

*   *   *

Close-up study of an historical problem is a chastening experience. One finds many surprises: likeable, or at least understandable, qualities in individuals or groups he expected to detest, curious disparities between intention and execution, comparisons where contrasts were anticipated. This was certainly true of the present study. The author began it in fair certainty that the Japanese annexation of Korea was essentially a question of timing, with Japanese leaders biding their time and waiting for a favorable opportunity. But instead of finding proof of this, he realized more and more how strong is the American disposition to see Japanese expansion (or that of another power) in terms of long-range, nefarious design, without being aware that our own not inconsiderable extraterritorial activities could appear quite as sinister, viewed from the outside with little attention to internal arguments, contradictions, and pressures.

SUGGESTIONS FOR ADDITIONAL READING

As yet, there is no single bibliography with convenient, detailed listings on Meiji expansionism and imperialism. What follows is an informal guide to some old and new works which offer further information and thoughts on the problem. Textbooks have not been included.

The best introduction to the specific issues of Meiji diplomacy is Marius B. Jansen, "Modernization and Foreign Policy in Meiji Japan," in *Political Development in Modern Japan*, ed. Robert E. Ward (Princeton, 1968), pp. 149–188. Other good surveys are Tōyama Shigeki, "Politics, Economics, and the International Environment in the Meiji and Taisho Periods," *The Developing Economies*, IV (December, 1966), pp. 419–446; Kimitada MIWA, "Fukuzawa Yukichi's 'Departure from Asia,' A Prelude to the Sino-Japanese War," in *Japan's Modern Century*, ed. Edmund Skrzpczak (Tokyo, 1968), pp. 1–26; and Akira IRIYE, "The Legacy of Modern Japanese Diplomacy," *Journal of Social and Political Ideas in Japan*, III (August, 1965), pp. 25–32. Hilary Conroy singles out dominant themes in "Government versus 'Patriot': The Background of Japan's Asiatic Expansion," *Pacific Historical Review*, XX (February, 1951), pp. 31–42, and settles on security of the frontier in "Lessons from Japanese Imperialism," *Monumenta Nipponica*, XXI (1966), pp. 333–345. Mushakoji Kimihide assesses the past century in an article as fascinating for its methodology as its contents: "From Fear of Dependence to Fear of Independence—A Senario of the Japanese International Learning Process," *Japan Annual of International Affairs*, no. 3 (1963–64), pp. 68–86.

For the controversial question of traditional expansionism, the standard work is Kuno Yoshisaburō, *Japanese Expansion on the Asiatic Continent*, 2 vols. (Berkeley, 1937–1940). Among the few specialized studies of the pre-Tokugawa centuries are Benjamin Hazard on pirates, "The Formative Years of the Wakō, 1223–63," *Monumenta Nipponica*, 22 (1967), pp. 260–277; Wang I-t'ung, *Official Relations between China and Japan, 1368–1549* (Harvard, 1953), and Mori Katsumi, "International Relations between the Tenth and the Sixteenth Century and the Development of the Japanese International Consciousness," *Acta Asiatica*, II (1961), pp. 69–98. Guiliana Stramigioli gives the most famous example of aggression in "Hideyoshi's Expansionist Policy on the Asiatic Mainland," *Transactions of the Asiatic Society of Japan*, 3rd series, III (December, 1954), pp. 74–16. Japanese ventures in East Asia and Southeast Asia before the era of seclusion and the reasons for adopting such a policy are discussed in C. R. Boxer, *The Christian Century in Japan, 1549–1650* (Berkeley, 1951). There are valuable readings on Tokugawa expansionist thought in *Sources of Japanese Tradition* (Columbia, 1958), chap. 22, "The Shinto Revival," and chap. 23, "Reformers of the Late Tokugawa Period." This is more extensively treated by Donald Keene in *The Japanese Discovery of Europe; 1720–1830* rev. ed. (Stanford, 1969). The last half of David Earl's *Emperor and Nation in Japan* (Seattle, 1964), is the best study in English of Yoshida Shōin. There is an excellent analysis of the *kaikoku-jōi* debates by William G. Beasley in his introduction to *Select Documents on Japanese Foreign Policy, 1853–1868* (London, 1955), pp. 1–93. Whether or not Japan was in much danger from the West in the 1860's may be determined by reading Gordon Daniels, "The British Role in the Meiji Restoration: A Re-Interpretive Note," *Modern Asian Studies, II*, part 4 (October, 1968), pp. 291–313; Meron Medzini, "Leon Roches in Japan (1864–1868)," *Papers on Japan*, II (Harvard, August 1963), pp. 182–228; and John McMaster, "Alcock and Harris: Foreign Diplomacy in Bakumatsu Japan," *Monumenta Nipponica*, XXII (1967), pp. 305–367.

The question of lingering feudal and military remnants and the special nature of Japan's modernization requires attention before examining the Meiji military and diplomatic establishments. An older view is Asakawa Kan'ichi, "Some of the Contributions of Feudal Japan to the New Japan," in *Japan and Japanese-American Relations*, ed. George H. Blakeslee (New York, 1912). More recent scholarship is reflected in *Studies in the Institutional History of Early Modern Japan*, edited by John W. Hall and Marius Jansen (Princeton, 1968), particularly contributions by John W. Hall, "The New Look of Tokugawa History," and Marius Jansen, "Tokugawa and Modern Japan." The term "modernization" gets a good workout from the same two scholars in chapters written for *Changing Japanese Attitudes toward Modernization* (Princeton, 1965), edited by Marius Jansen. A survey of Japanese modernization which is very critical of the "success thesis" is the chapter entitled "Asian Fascism: Japan," in Barrington Moore, *Social Origins of Dictatorship and Democracy* (Boston, 1966), pp. 228–313.

For the making of Meiji Japan's modern military establishment, see Hyman Kublin, "The Modern Army of Early Meiji Japan," *Far Eastern Quarterly*, IX (November, 1949), pp. 255–66; Ernst Presseisen, *Before Aggression, Europeans Prepare the Japanese Army* (Tucson, 1965); Fukushima Shingo, "The Building of a National Army," in *Studies in the Modernization of Japan*, I, ed. Tōbata Seiichi (Tokyo, 1966); Roger Hackett, "The Military: Japan," in *Political Modernization in Japan and Turkey*, eds. Robert E. Ward and D. A. Rustow (Princeton, 1964), pp. 328–351; and John C. Perry, "Great Britain and the Emergence of Japan as a Naval Power," *Monumenta Nipponica*, XXI (1966), pp. 305–321. An influential interpretation of *bushidō*, before it became identified as the code of fanatical Japanese soldiers in the Pacific War, may be found in *Bushidō* by Nitobe Inazo (New York, 1905). See also the previously cited works by Tsunoda, Earl, and Asakawa.

The theory and practice of the Chinese world order, which the West and then Japan sought to replace in East Asia, is analyzed in John K. Fairbank, *Trade and Diplomacy on the China Coast* (Cambridge, 1953), vol. I, pp. 3–53. One of Japan's most important initial sources of information on international law was a Chinese translation in 1864 of a standard Western text. See Immanual C. Y. Hsü, *China's Entrance into the Family of Nations* (Cambridge, 1960), pp. 121–131. There is as yet no comparable volume for the Japanese case, but Ōhira Zengo's "Japan's Reception of the Law of Nations," *The Annals of the Hitotsubashi Academy*, IV (October, 1953), pp. 55–66, contains some information. There is a good summary of Fukuzawa Yukichi's changing attitudes toward international law by Carmen Blacker in *The Japanese Enlightenment* (Cambridge, 1964), chap. 9 (The New Comity of Nations). William Langer's *The Diplomacy of Imperialism, 1890–1902*, 2nd ed. (New York, 1951), chaps. 6, 12, 14, and 21, is still the standard treatment of Japan's diplomatic and military maneuvers at the end of the century. It should be supplemented by Takeuchi Tatsuji, *War and Diplomacy in the Japanese Empire* (New York, 1935); Akira IRIYE, *Across the Pacific* (New York, 1967), chaps. 3–4; and Frank W. Iklé, "The Triple Intervention: Japan's Lesson in the Diplomacy of Imperialism," *Monumenta Nipponica*, XXII (1967), pp. 122–130.

There are several books and articles which together give a fairly detailed description of Japan's initial expansion as an imperial power. The conflicting interests of Japan and Russia in Hokkaido, the Kuriles, and Sakhalin are best described in *The Russian Push toward Japan, Russo-Japanese Relations, 1697–1875*, by George A. Lensen (Princeton, 1959). Lensen has written a short account of the post-1875 period in "Japan and Tsarist Russia—the Changing Relationships, 1875–1917," *Jahrbücher für Geshichte Osteuropas*, X (October, 1962), pp. 337–347. John A. Harrison's *Japan's Northern Frontier* (Gainesville, 1953) examines the colonization of Hokkaido. The extension of the southern frontier to include the Ryukyu Islands is described in George H. Kerr, *Okinawa, The History of An Island People* (Rutland, 1958). Japan's interests in the islands before the Meiji era is further explained by Robert Sakai in "The Ryukyu (Liu-Ch'iu) Islands as a Fief of Satsuma," in *The Chinese World Order*, ed. John K. Fairbank (Cambridge, 1968), pp. 112–134. Hyman Kublin traces the Sino-Japanese negotiations for the islands in "The Attitude of China during the Liu-Ch'iu Controversy, 1871–81," *Pacific Historical Review*, XVIII (May, 1949), pp. 213–31. Kublin's article also illustrates Japan's early acceptance of international law.

There is only one full-length study of Japan and the Philippines in the Meiji period, Josefa Saniel's *Japan and the Philippines, 1868–1898* (Quezon City, 1962). Also useful in assessing the extent of Meiji Japan's imperial ambitions are Hilary Conroy, *The Japanese Frontier in Hawaii, 1868–1898* (Berkeley, 1953) and T. A. Bailey, "Japan's Protest against the Annexation of Hawaii," *Journal of Modern History*, III (1931), pp. 46–61.

Formosa and Korea are both very tangled questions. It is best to begin with a general account of relations between China and Japan in the Meiji period, such as T. F. Tsiang, "Sino-Japanese Diplomatic Relations, 1870–1894," *The Chinese Social and Political Science Review*, XVII (April, 1933), pp. 1–106 and Marius B. Jansen, "Japanese Views of China during the Meiji Period," in *Approaches to Modern Chinese History*, ed. Albert Fuerwerker, *et al.* (Berkeley, 1967), pp. 163–189. Another essay by Akira IRIYE is very good although most of his remarks pertain to the post-1912 years: "The Ideology of Japanese Imperialism: Imperial Japan and China," in *Imperial Japan and Asia, A Reassessment*, ed. Grant Goodman, Occasional Papers of the East Asian Institute, Columbia University (1967), pp. 32–45. The Formosan expedition of 1874 is seen as evidence of the will to expand by Leonard Gordon, "Japan's Abortive Colonial Venture in Taiwan, 1874," *Journal of Modern History*, XXXVII (June,

1965), pp. 171–185. The domestic pressures which helped produce this decision are given in Masakazu IWATA, *Ōkubo Toshimichi, The Bismarck of Japan* (Berkeley, 1964), pp. 184–225. The most exhaustive, meticulous study is Sophia Su-fei Yen's *Taiwan in China's Foreign Relations, 1836–1874* (Hamden, Connecticut, 1965). Leonard Gordon has dealt with the Taiwan problem over a longer period in "Japan's Interest in Taiwan, 1872–1895," *Orient/West*, X (Jan.–Feb., 1969), pp. 49–59. Additional information on the subsequent acquisition of Formosa is in F. Q. Quo, "British Diplomacy and the Cession of Formosa, 1894–95," *Modern Asian Studies*, II, Part 2 (October, 1968), pp. 141–154. More recent studies of the initial colonial policy include Chang Han-yu and Ramon H. Myers, "Japanese Colonial Development Policy in Taiwan, 1895–1906: A Case of Bureaucratic Entrepreneurship," *Journal of Asian Studies*, XXII (August, 1968), pp. 433–449, and two essays in *Papers on Japan*, IV (Harvard, 1967): E. Patricia Tsurumi, "Taiwan under Kodama Gentarō and Gotō Shimpei," and Ching-chih CHEN, "The Police and Hokō Sytems in Taiwan under Japanese Administration (1895–1945)."

For the issues at stake in the Korean debate, 1873, there is Nobutaka IKE's "The Crisis of 1873," chap. 5, in *The Beginnings of Political Democracy in Japan* (Baltimore, 1950), which complements his "Triumph of the Peace Party in Japan in 1873," *Far Eastern Quarterly*, II (May, 1943), pp. 286–295. Two recent books which both augment and counter Conroy's arguments are *Korea and the Politics of Imperialism, 1876–1910* (Berkeley, 1967) by C. I. Eugene Kim and Han-kyo Kim, and Frederick Foo Chien, *The Opening of Korea* (Shoe String Press, 1967). Andrew Nahm gives a balanced assessment of Japan's Korean Policy in "Reaction and Response to the Opening of Korea, 1876–1884," in *Studies on Asia, 1965*, ed. Robert Sakai (Lincoln, 1965), pp. 61–80. The interest of early Japanese liberals in Korea is analyzed by Marius Jansen in "Ōi Kentaro: Radicalism and Chauvinism," *Far*

Eastern Quarterly, XI (May, 1952), pp. 305–316.

The Sino-Japanese and Russo-Japanese wars have received surprisingly little attention in Western literature. Besides Langer and Takeuchi, there is also Payson J. Treat, who explains Japan's case in "The Cause of the Sino-Japanese War, 1894," *Pacific Historical Review*, VIII (June, 1939), pp. 149–157. Ernest P. Young uses the approach of decision-making in "A Study of Groups and Personalities in Japan Influencing the Events Leading to the Sino-Japanese War (1894–1895)," *Papers on Japan*, II (Harvard, 1963), pp. 229–275. Ian Nish describes how Russia replaced China as Japan's chief worry in "Korea, Focus of Russo-Japanese Diplomacy (1898–1903)," *Asian Studies*, IV (April, 1966), pp. 70–83. On the growing rivalry in Manchuria there is Charles Nelson Spinks, "Origins of Japanese Interests in Manchuria," *Far Eastern Quarterly*, II (May, 1943), pp. 259–72, and Paul H. Clyde, *International Rivalries in Manchuria* (Columbus, 1926). John Albert White shows how Japan became involved in and then got out of the war with Russia in *The Diplomacy of the Russo-Japanese War* (Princeton, 1964). For Russia's aims, see Andrew Malozemoff, *Russian Far Eastern Policy, 1881–1904, with Special Emphasis on the Causes of the Russo-Japanese War* (Berkeley, 1958). Other signs of possible imperial ambition at the turn of the century are discussed by Ian Nish, "Japan's Indecision during the Boxer Disturbances," *Journal of Asian Studies*, XX (August, 1961), pp. 449–461, and Marius Jansen, "Opportunists in South China during the Boxer Rebellion," *Pacific Historical Review*, XX (August, 1951), pp. 241–250. A very extensive and recent study on the first Anglo-Japanese Alliance and attendant complications is Ian Nish, *The Anglo-Japanese Alliance, The Diplomacy of Two Island Empires, 1894–1907* (London, 1966). Several works on Theodore Roosevelt and Japan contain valuable clues to Japan's reasons for expansion; among them are Tyler Dennett, *Roosevelt and the Russo-Japanese War* (New York,

1925); Raymond A. Esthus, *Theodore Roosevelt and Japan* (Seattle, 1966); and Charles E. Neu, *An Uncertain Friendship, Theodore Roosevelt and Japan, 1906–1909* (Cambridge, 1967). However, many of the issues have yet to be thoroughly explored from Japanese documents.

On the general problem of Meiji nationalism there is Delmar Brown's *Nationalism in Japan* (Berkeley, 1955), chaps. 5–8. D. C. Holtom's *Modern Japan and Shinto Nationalism* rev. ed. (New York, 1947) is relevant mainly to the post-1912 period. More to the point is Hilary Conroy's "Japanese Nationalism and Expansionism," *American Historical Review*, LX (July, 1955), pp. 818–829. Herbert Passin indicates the use of Meiji education for political indoctrination in *Society and Education in Japan* (New York, 1965), chaps. 4 and 7. John Embree suggests that Japanese national attitudes and myths may not be much more extreme or ultrapatriotic than those of other people in *The Japanese Nation, A Social Survey* (New York, 1945). *The Developing Economies* has been publishing a series of articles recently on the theme of Asian-minded men; among them are Keizō IKIMATSU on Okakura Tenshin, IV (December, 1966); Sannosuke MATSUMOTO on Fukuzawa Yukichi, V (March, 1967); Tōru MIYAKAWA and Takeru IGETA on Tokutomo Sohō, V (September, 1967); and Tadashi SUZUKI on Tarui Tokichi, VI (March, 1968). Other authors who develop the theme of nationalism and expansionism by examining the thought of influential persons are Albert Craig, "Fukuzawa Yukichi: The Philosophical Foundations of Meiji Nationalism," in *Political Development in Modern Japan*, ed. Robert E. Ward (Princeton, 1968), pp. 99–148; Barbara Teters on Kuga Katsunan in "A Liberal Nationalist and the Meiji Constitution," *Studies on Asia*, ed. by Robert Sakai (Lincoln, 1965), pp. 105–123; and Marlene Mayo, "Attitudes toward Asia and the Beginnings of Japanese Empire," in Goodman, pp. 6–31. There are very few sources on critics of empire building other than Hyman Kublin's "The Japanese Socialists and the

Russo-Japanese War," *Journal of Modern History*, XXII (December, 1950) and scattered comments in Kōsaka Masaaki, *Japanese Thought in the Meiji Period* (Tokyo, 1958).

Although there are many general studies and several specialized ones on the development of Japan's modern economy, few comment extensively on the question of Meiji capitalism and imperialism. Generalizations are overly casual, making it difficult to know what happened when or why. Of some help are William Lockwood, *The Economic Development of Japan, Growth and Structural Change, 1863–1938* (Princeton, 1954) and William Lockwood, ed., *The State and Economic Enterprise in Japan* (Princeton, 1965). Ronald Dore's chapter on "Tenancy and Aggression" in *Land Reform in Japan* (Oxford, 1959) raises again the issue of "success" or "failure" in achieving modernization. At whose expense was Japan modernized? Almost all of the articles in the special issue of *The Developing Economies*, subtitled "The Modernization of Japan—II," IV (December, 1966) are of interest. Very useful in determining the motives of the Meiji business community is Byron K. Marshall, *Capitalism and Nationalism in Prewar Japan, The Ideology of the Business Elite, 1868–1941* (Stanford, 1967).

The assumption that Japan was inherently expansionist goes unquestioned in many of the essays cited above, perhaps because they were written after the aggression of the 1930's. It might therefore be best to recommend in closing a few works which indicate how Western contemporaries viewed the expansionist activities of Meiji Japan. Two Americans who knew first hand about the Formosan expedition, 1874, were the journalist Edward H. House, who accompanied the Japanese army and wrote *The Japanese Expedition to Formosa* (Tokyo, 1875), and Charles W. LeGendre, an adviser to the Japanese Foreign Ministry and author of *Progressive Japan: A Study in the Political and Social Needs of the Empire* (1878). Charles Lanman, who was employed in Japan's Washington legation, supported Japanese claims to the Ryukyus in "The Islands of Okinawa," *International Review*, VII (1880), pp. 18–27. Two books which are particularly interesting because their authors, both Englishmen, made the Asian grand tour and compared Japan to the rest of Asia are: C. N. Curzon, *Problems of the Far East: Japan, Korea, China* 2nd ed. (London, 1896), and Valentine Chirol, *The Far Eastern Question* (London, 1896). The diaries of Sir Ernest Satow yield perceptive observations on the sources of Russo-Japanese tension; see *Korea and Manchuria between Russia and Japan, 1895–1904*, edited by George A. Lensen (Tallahassee, 1966). There are some passing references to the yellow peril, Chinese and Japanese, in Isaac Don Levine, *The Kaiser's Letters to the Tsar* (London, 1928). In the United States few lamented or were surprised by Japan's annexation of Korea in 1910. See William Elliot Griffis, "Japan's Absorption of Korea," *North American Review*, 192 (October, 1910), pp. 516–526, and George Trumbull Ladd, "The Annexation of Korea: An Essay in 'Benevolent Assimilation,' " *Yale Review*, vol. I, new series (July, 1912), pp. 639–656. Among the few detractors were the missionary Homer Hulbert, *The Passing of Korea* (New York, 1906) and F. A. McKenzie, *Tragedy of Korea* (New York, 1908). For Willard Straight's cries of alarm see Herbert Croly, *Willard Straight* (New York, 1924).

Finally, the Japanese pleaded their own case quite effectively. Examples are: Asakawa Kan'ichi in *The Russo-Japanese Conflict, Its Causes and Issues* (Boston, 1904); Hishida Seiji, *The International Position of Japan as a Great Power* (New York, 1905); Iyenaga Toyokichi, "Japan's Annexation of Korea," in Blakeslee, pp. 275–297; and Nitobe Inazo, "Japanese Colonization," *Asiatic Review*, XVI (1920), pp. 113–121.

WITHDRAWN